READY TO LEARN

Kindergarten

Workbook

Table of Contents

READY TO LEARN

Kindergarten

A NOTE TO PARENTS, CAREGIVERS, AND TEACHERS

The *Ready to Learn* series is an excellent tool for assisting your child, grandchild, or student in developing readiness skills in mathematics, reading, and writing during his or her early learning years. The colorful and engaging workbooks, workpads, and flash cards support the acquisition of foundational skills that all children need to be successful in school and everyday life.

The *Ready to Learn* series develops skills targeted to the Common Core State Standards. The practice workbooks include explanations, strategies, and practice opportunities that engage your young learner with the building blocks needed to become a confident mathematician, reader, and writer. The workpads provide additional practice for the key concepts addressed in the workbooks, and the flash cards support fluency in basic math and reading concepts.

Ready to Learn workbooks include an overview page to inform adults of the learning objectives inside, as well as a certificate at the end of the book to present to your child or student upon completion of the workbook. It is recommended that you display each certificate earned in a prominent location where your child or student can proudly share with others that he or she is excited to be a learner!

While the *Ready to Learn* series is designed to support your child's or student's acquisition of foundational skills, it is important that you practice these skills beyond the series. Encourage your child or student to find examples of what he or she has learned in various environments, such as letters and words on menus at a restaurant, numbers at a grocery store, and colors and shapes on the playground.

Thank you for caring about your child or student's education.
Happy learning!

# Reading

Table of Contents

Kindergarten Reading Readiness

Children can learn the ABC song at a very early age, but surprisingly, letter recognition and letter sounds are better taught in a different order. Teaching the letters and sounds that in combination form sight words and familiar phonics patterns will boost a child's ability to read faster. Reading can be a fun time to connect with your child every day. Cuddle up and read to your child as often as possible.

As you complete the activities in this book with your child, be sure to point to the words as you read them aloud. This helps with one-on-one correlation as your child listens. Also, be sure to say the sounds of the letters rather than the letter names as you work on pages 5 to 30 and the combination sounds on pages 31 to 35.

Learning letters and sounds with rhymes and actions makes learning fun!

Letter S

Say, "Snake, snake, S...S...S," while making a slithery snake motion with your hand.

Practice writing the letters on the lines below. Say the sound as you write.

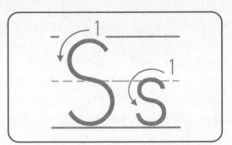

Write the beginning sound for each word below.

___ nake   ___ nail   ___ wan

Letter A

Say, "Apple, apple, A...A...A," while pretending to hold an apple in your hand and bringing it to your mouth.

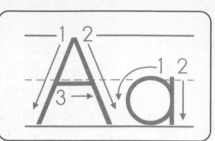

Practice writing the letters on the lines below.
Say the sound as you write.

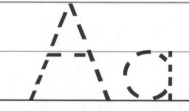

Write the beginning sound for each word below.

 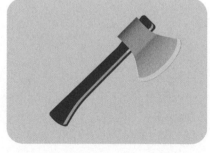 

_____ pple   _____ x   _____ corn

Letter T

Say, "Tiger, tiger, T...T...T," while making claws with your hands and roaring.

Practice writing the letters on the lines below.
Say the sound as you write.

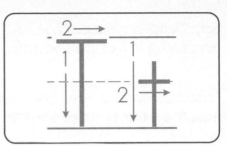

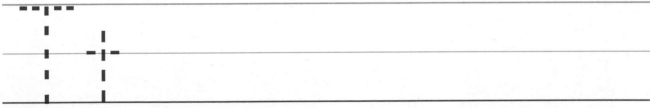

Write the beginning sound for each word below.

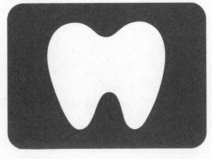

_____ iger   _____ ooth   _____ urtle

7

Letter I

Say, "Iguana, iguana, I...I...I," while sticking your tongue out like an iguana.

Practice writing the letters on the lines below. Say the sound as you write.

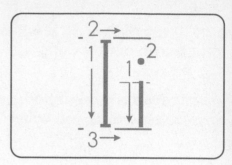

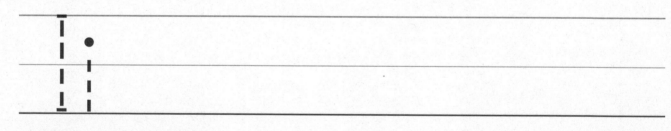

Write the beginning sound for each word below.

_____ guana _____ nsect _____ ce

Letter P

Say, "Pig, pig, P...P...P," while scrunching your nose up like a pig.

Practice writing the letters on the lines below. Say the sound as you write.

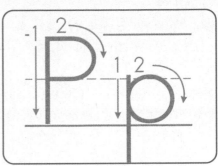

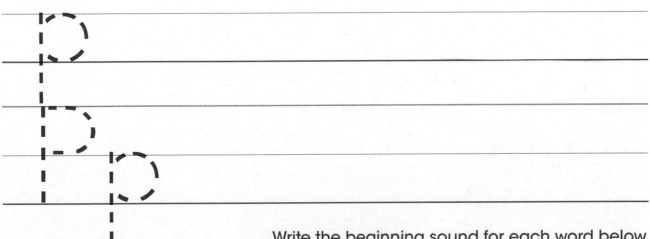

Write the beginning sound for each word below.

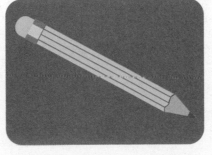

___ig ___encil ___ail

Letter N

Say, "Night, night, N...N...N," while closing your eyes and pretending to sleep.

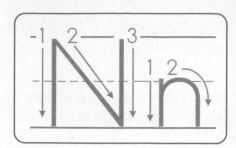

Practice writing the letters on the lines below.
Say the sound as you write.

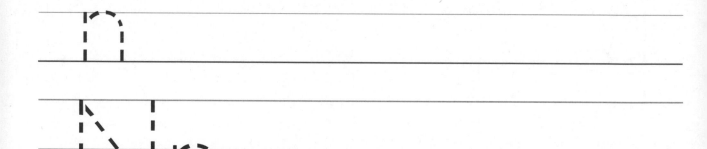

Write the beginning sound for each word below.

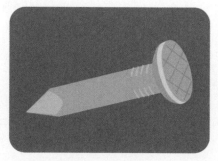

_____ ight   _____ ail   _____ est

10

Letter C

Say, "Crab, crab, C...C...C," while pretending to make crab claws with your hands.

Practice writing the letters on the lines below. Say the sound as you write.

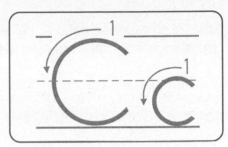

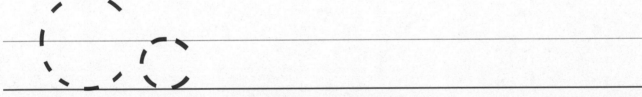

Write the beginning sound for each word below.

___ rab   ___ at   ___ oat

Letter K

Say, "Koala, koala, K...K...K," while putting your arms together like you're hugging a tree.

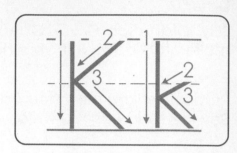

Practice writing the letters on the lines below. Say the sound as you write.

Write the beginning sound for each word below.

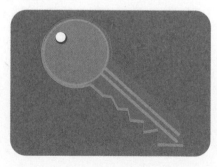

____ oala   ____ ey   ____ ite

Letter E

Say, "Elbow, elbow, E...E...E," while bringing your hands to your chest and flapping your arms like wings.

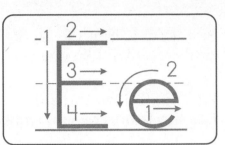

Practice writing the letters on the lines below.
Say the sound as you write.

Write the beginning sound for each word below.

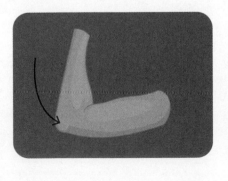

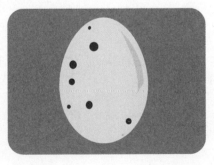

_____ lbow

_____ gg

_____ agle

13

Letter H

Say, "Hand, hand, H...H...H," while waving your hands high in the air.

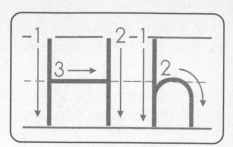

Practice writing the letters on the lines below. Say the sound as you write.

Write the beginning sound for each word below.

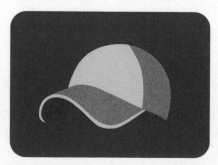

_____ and

_____ at

_____ orse

14

Letter R

Say, "Rabbit, rabbit, R...R...R," while making rabbit ears with your hands and hopping like a rabbit.

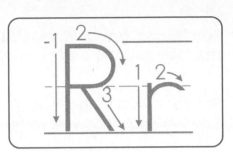

Practice writing the letters on the lines below. Say the sound as you write.

R

r

Rr

Write the beginning sound for each word below.

____ abbit

____ obot

____ ecycle

Letter M

Say, "Monkey, monkey, M...M...M," while making monkey sounds and bouncing around.

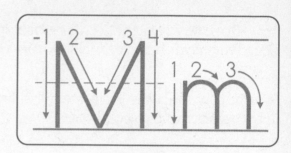

Practice writing the letters on the lines below. Say the sound as you write.

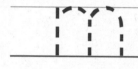

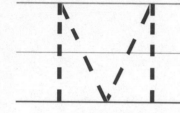

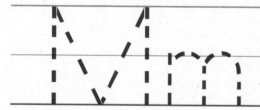

Write the beginning sound for each word below.

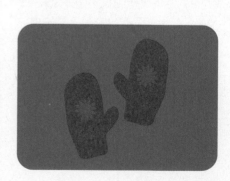

_____ onkey　　_____ oon　　_____ ittens

Letter D

Say, "Dog, dog, D...D...D," while barking like a dog.

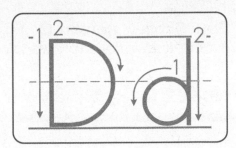

Practice writing the letters on the lines below.
Say the sound as you write.

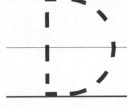

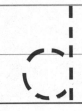

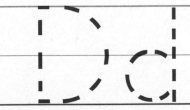

Write the beginning sound for each word below.

_____ og   _____ olphin   _____ rum

Letter G

Say, "Garden, garden, G...G...G," while pretending to smell flowers you have picked.

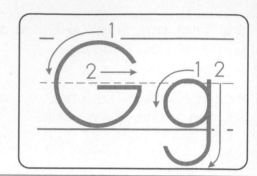

Practice writing the letters on the lines below. Say the sound as you write.

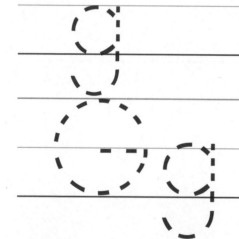

Write the beginning sound for each word below.

_____ arden   _____ oat   _____ iraffe

Letter O

Say, "Octopus, octopus, O...O...O," while wiggling your arms like tentacles.

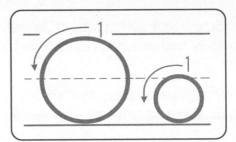

Practice writing the letters on the lines below. Say the sound as you write.

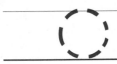

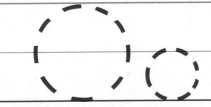

Write the beginning sound for each word below.

_____ ctopus   _____ strich   _____ val

19

Letter L

Say, "Lion, lion, L...L...L," while making your hands look like paws and roaring.

Practice writing the letters on the lines below. Say the sound as you write.

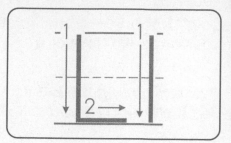

Write the beginning sound for each word below.

_____ ion   _____ eaf   _____ izard

Letter F

Say, "Flower, flower, F...F...F," while opening your fingers like a flower.

Practice writing the letters on the lines below. Say the sound as you write.

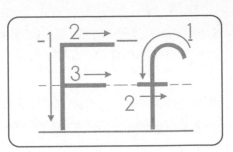

Write the beginning sound for each word below.

_____ lower _____ ish _____ lag

Letter Sounds

Letter B

Say, "Baby, baby, B...B...B," while pretending you're rocking a baby.

Practice writing the letters on the lines below. Say the sound as you write.

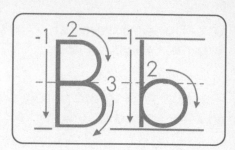

Write the beginning sound for each word below.

_____ aby   _____ ear   _____ all

Letter Q

Say, "Queen, queen, Q...Q...Q," while pretending to put a crown on your head.

Practice writing the letters on the lines below.
Say the sound as you write.

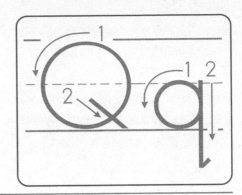

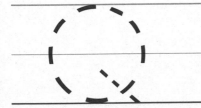

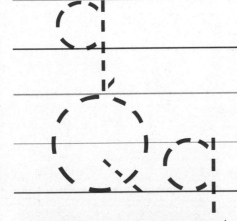

Write the beginning sound for each word below.

_____ ueen   _____ uail   _____ uilt

Letter U

Say, "Unicorn, unicorn, U...U...U," while prancing like a unicorn.

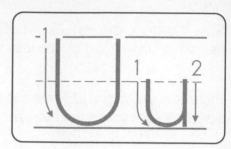

Practice writing the letters on the lines below. Say the sound as you write.

Write the beginning sound for each word below.

_____ nicorn

_____ mbrella

Letter J

Say, "Jump, jump, J...J...J," while jumping up and down.

Practice writing the letters on the lines below. Say the sound as you write.

Write the beginning sound for each word below.

_____ ump   _____ uice   _____ acket

Letter Z

Say, "Zebra, zebra, Z...Z...Z," while galloping like a zebra.

Practice writing the letters on the lines below.
Say the sound as you write.

Write the beginning sound for each word below.

_____ ebra   _____ ipper   _____ igzag

Letter W

Say, "Worm, worm, W...W...W," while lying on the ground pretending to move like a worm.

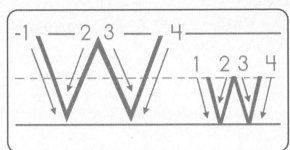

Practice writing the letters on the lines below. Say the sound as you write.

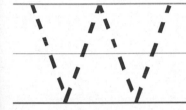

Write the beginning sound for each word below.

___ orm   ___ alrus   ___ agon

Letter V

Say, "Violin, violin, V...V...V," while pretending to play a violin.

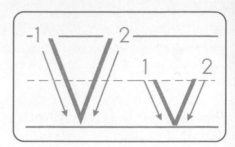

Practice writing the letters on the lines below.
Say the sound as you write.

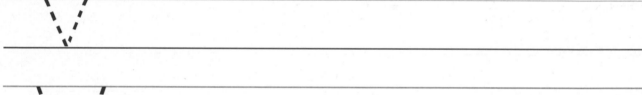

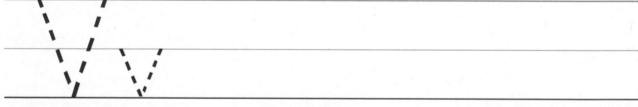

Write the beginning sound for each word below.

_____ iolin   _____ olcano   _____ an

Letter Y

Say, "Yo-yo, yo-yo, Y...Y...Y," while pretending to play with a yo-yo.

Practice writing the letters on the lines below. Say the sound as you write.

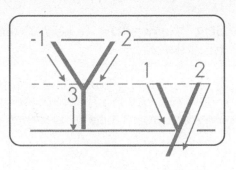

Write the beginning sound for each word below.

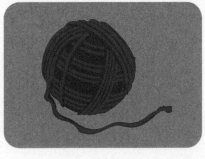

___ o-yo   ___ arn   ___ ellow

Letter X

Say, "X-ray, x-ray, X...X...X," while pretending to take an x-ray.

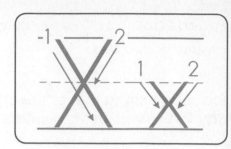

Practice writing the letters on the lines below. Say the sound as you write.

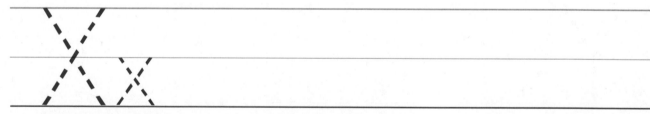

Write the missing sound for each word below.

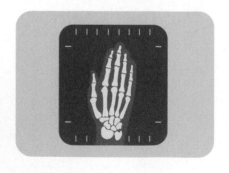  

_____ -ray   bo _____   fo _____

Letter Combinations

Sometimes a combination of letters makes one sound. Practice saying these sounds and building words with letter combinations.

sh and th

Say, "s...h...sh...sh...sh," while putting your finger to your lips when you say the "sh" sound.

Say, "t...h...th...th...th," while putting your tongue between your teeth to make the sound.

Practice writing the letter combinations on the lines below.
Say the sounds as you write.

sh

th

Write the missing letter combination for each word below.

____ ip   fi ____   ba ____

Letter Combinations

ch and wh

Say, "c...h...ch...ch...ch," while making your arms look like wings and flapping them like a chicken.

Say, "w...h...wh...wh...wh," while moving your arm like you are spinning a wheel.

Practice writing the letter combinations on the lines below.
Say the sounds as you write.

Write the beginning letter combination for each word below.

___ eel   ___ eek   ___ ale

32

ing

Say, "i...n...g...ing...ing...ing," while jumping in a circle.

Practice writing the letter combination on the lines below.
Say the sound as you write.

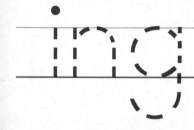

Write the ending letter combination for each word below.

S _____

W _____

r _____

sw _____

33

er

Say, "e...r...er...er...er," while you spread your fingers to make your hand look like a flower.

Practice writing the letter combination on the lines below.
Say the sound as you write.

Write the ending letter combination for each word below.

flow _____

moth _____

wat _____

sist _____

ar

Say, "a...r...ar...ar...ar," while you put your hand over one eye like a pirate's eye patch.

Practice writing the letter combination on the lines below.
Say the sound as you write.

Write the missing letter combination for each word below.

c _____

st _____

j _____

p_____ k

35

Word Families

Teaching word families can help children recognize patterns in words and learn how to build new words with these patterns. This essential part of beginner reading can be fun and will lead to an understanding of how words rhyme.

Try singing or reading nursery rhymes with your child. Point out how some of the words sound the same.

wish

dish

fish

-at

What words are in the -at word family?

Build new words with the -at word family. Fill in the missing letters to complete the words. Then color the pictures.

_____ _____ ___at

_____ _____ ___at

_____ _____ ___at

_____ _____ ___at

_____ _____ ___at

-en

What words are in the -en word family?

Build new words with the -en word family. Fill in the missing word family to complete the words. Then color the pictures.

h_____

p_____

d_____

t_____

m_____

Word Families

-op

What words are in the -op word family?

Build new words with the -op word family. Fill in the missing letters to complete the words on the -op train.

-ig

What words are in the -ig word family?

Build new words with the -ig word family. Fill in the missing word family to complete the words. Then color the pictures.

ig

p _____

w _____

d _____

j _____

-ug

What words are in the -ug word family?

Build new words with the -ug word family. Fill in the missing letters to complete the words. Then color the pictures.

_____ ug

_____ ug

_____ ug

_____ ug

_____ ug

-ap

What words are in the -ap word family?

Build new words with the -ap word family. Fill in the missing word family to complete the words. Then color the pictures.

_____

c_____

_____

m_____

_____

n_____

_____

sn_____

_____

cl_____

-ot

What words are in the -ot word family?

Build new words with the -ot word family. Color the pictures that show words that have the -ot sound in them. Look for hot, dot, and pot.

Phonics is an important building block for learning to read. Children need to practice connecting a letter to the sound it makes, and then connecting a series of sounds to a series of letters that form a word. This begins with words that have three letters and three sounds, such as cat or dog. Then children can expand to words that have more letters than sounds, such as "tree," which has four letters but only three sounds.

Look at each picture and say the sounds. Trace the missing letter to complete the word and then color the pictures.

log

fin

hat

Phonics

Beginning Sound and Letter

What beginning sound do you hear? Write the beginning letter that matches both pictures on the lines below.

Middle Sounds

Say the word for each picture. Listen for the sound you hear in the middle. Circle the letter that makes that sound.

U
B
R

R
S
A

N
O
Y

T
I
L

P
E
R

F
I
U

Ending Sounds

Say the word for each picture. Listen for the sound you hear at the end. Write the letter that makes that sound on the lines below.

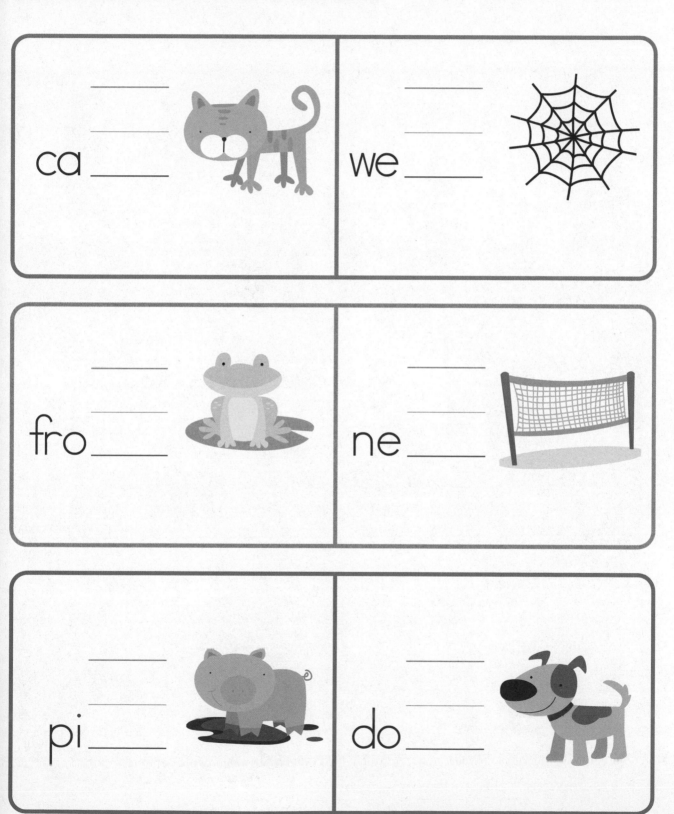

ca _____

we _____

fro _____

ne _____

pi _____

do _____

47

Reading Rhymes

Reading rhyming words helps children recognize the patterns in the words they see. It is great to read rhyming books with your child.

moose

truck

goose

duck

Match the Rhymes

Draw a line to match the words that rhyme. Then color the pictures.

Sun

Fan

Wish

Mop

Pan

Wig

Top

Fun

Pig

Fish

Reading Rhymes

Find the Rhyme

Circle the picture that rhymes with the picture on the left.

Write a word on the lines below that rhymes with the picture.

Find the Rhyme

Circle the words in the picture that rhyme with the word hat. Then color the hat.

HAT

mat

map

pig

man

cat

bat

pan

hop

fat

dog

dig

jog

sun

hen

fan

pat

van

sat

yak

rat

Write a word on the lines below that rhymes with the picture.

Sight Words

Sight words are high-frequency words, meaning you see them often in books. They can also be words that do not follow phonetic patterns and are difficult to sound out. Sight words need to be practiced and memorized so they are recognized as soon as children see them in a book. Use the sight words on the following pages to practice memorizing.

Come with me!

Look at him play ball.

She is very kind.

I like school.

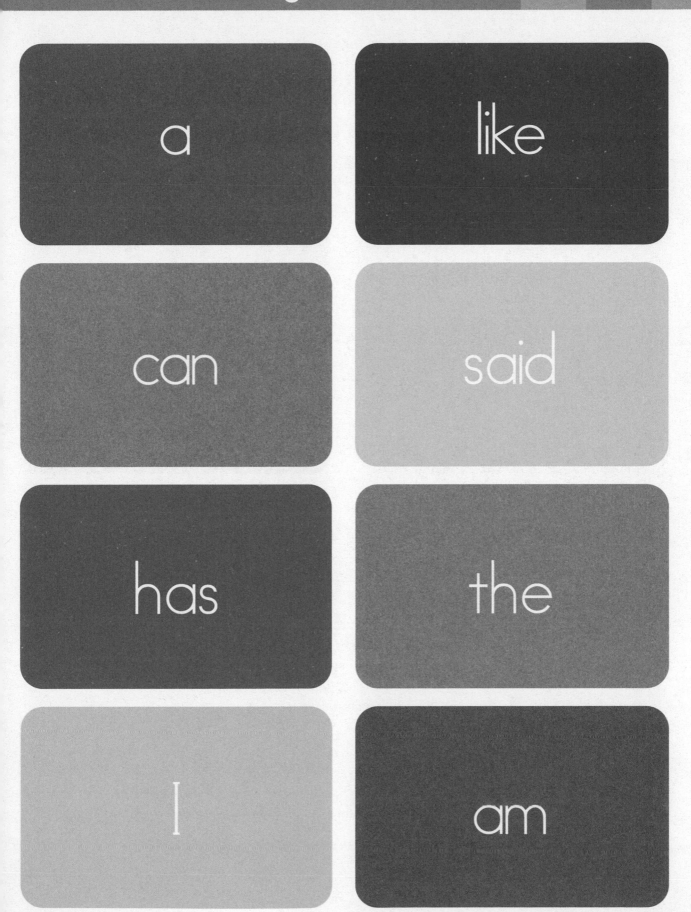

a

like

can

said

has

the

I

am

do

see

have

to

in

an

look

for

he

up

is

and

me

go

she

her

it

are

my

no

so

you

we

play

Sight Word Games

Follow the directions below.

Read the sight words.

see like me the to

Find and circle the sight words below.

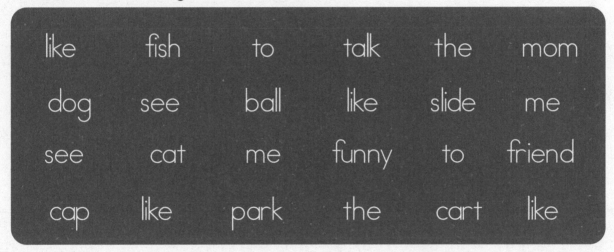

like	fish	to	talk	the	mom
dog	see	ball	like	slide	me
see	cat	me	funny	to	friend
cap	like	park	the	cart	like

Write the sight words you circled on the lines below.

_____

_____

_____

_____

_____

Practice writing sight words on the lines below.

look

like

play

Write the sight words from above in the sentences below.

I _____ dogs!

I can _____ out the window.

Will you come and _____ with me?

Sight Word Games

Color the picture using the key below.

green = and   blue = see   red = me

purple = to   orange = up   yellow = no

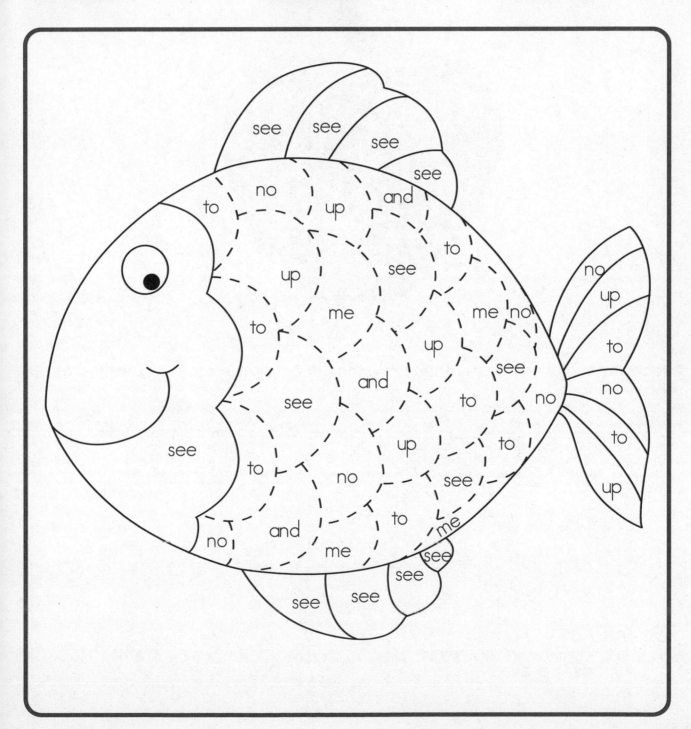

Time to Read!

It is important that a child understands what she or he is reading, even from a young age. Ask your child questions about what is happening in the story as you read. Reading and talking about what you read can become a great way to connect with your child.

Read the sentences below. Then circle the correct answers to the questions about the sentences.

I like to eat apples.
They are good for me.

1. What do you like to eat?

   • I like to eat apples.

   • I like to eat oranges.

2. Why do you eat them?

   • They are sweet.

   • They are good for me.

Time to Read!

Read the sentences below. Then circle the correct answers to the questions about the sentences.

I can go out to play.
It is fun!

1. What can you do?
    *   I can go out to play.
    *   I can ride a bike.

2. Why do you play?
    *   I like it.
    *   It is fun!

Time to Read!

Read the sentences below. Then circle the correct answers to the questions about the sentences.

> I see a dog.
> The dog ran away.

1. What do you see?
   - I see a cat.
   - I see a dog.

2. What did the dog do?
   - The dog ran away.
   - The dog barked.

Time to Read!

Read the sentences below. Then circle the correct answers to the questions about the sentences.

We are at the beach.
I'm playing in the sand.

1. Where are we?
   - We are at school.
   - We are at the beach.

2. What are you doing?
   - I'm playing in the sand.
   - I'm swimming.

CERTIFICATE
of Achievement

has successfully completed

Kindergarten Reading

Signed:

Date:

Writing

Table of Contents

Learning to write letters, words, and sentences can be challenging. It requires fine motor skills to be developed and visual spatial abilities to be fine-tuned. Handwriting should be taught in developmental order, beginning with uppercase letters followed by lowercase letters. There are lots of fun fine motor activities you can do with your child along the way.

Pipe Cleaners and Buttons

Put the pipe cleaners through the holes in the buttons. String as many as you can. Make them into bracelets and necklaces for fun!

Fine Motor Activity

Practicing Proper Pencil Grip

A-OK Grip

Have your child make an "ok" sign with his or her fingers. Have your child open his or her index finger and thumb slightly and then pinch the pencil with his or her first finger and thumb and fold the other fingers under. This works for children who are left-handed or right-handed.

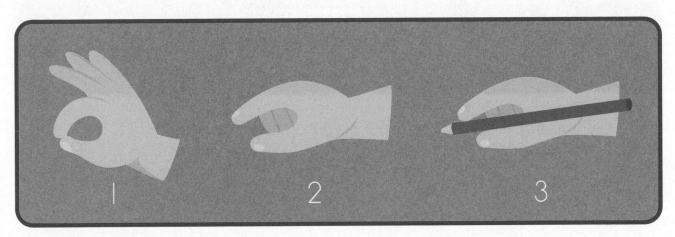

Flip the Pencil Trick

Have your child pick up a pencil with his or her first two fingers and thumb. Be sure to have your child pick it up close to the tip of the pencil.

Maintaining his or her grip, have your child use his or her other hand to flip the pencil around until it is in the proper position.

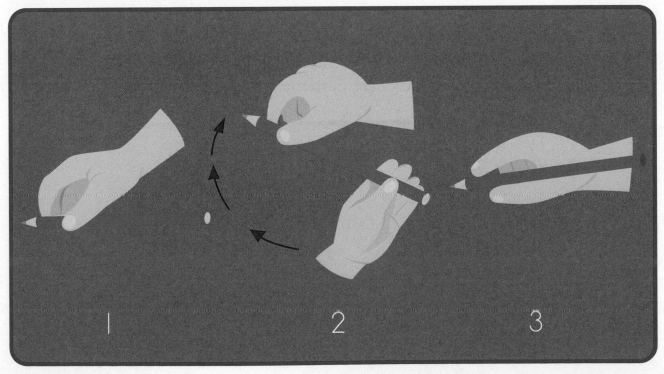

Letter F

Trace the uppercase letter F with your finger.

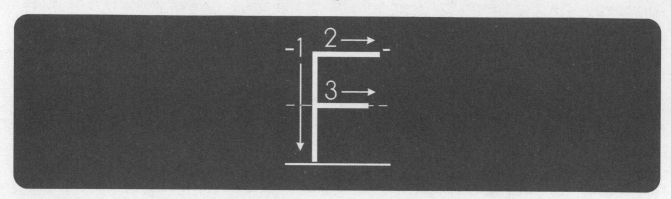

Trace the uppercase letter F with your pencil on the lines below.

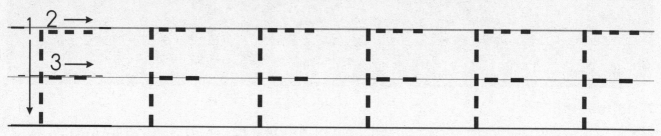

Practice writing the uppercase letter F on the lines below.

Draw a picture of something that starts with the letter F, such as a fox or a friend.

Letter E

Trace the uppercase letter E with your finger.

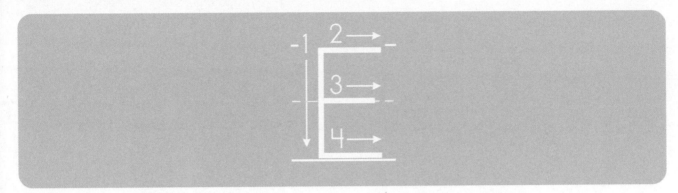

Trace the uppercase letter E with your pencil on the lines below.

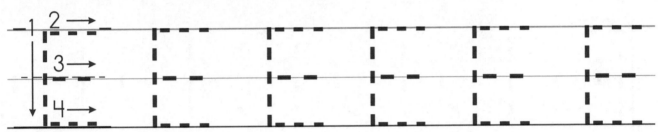

Practice writing the uppercase letter E on the lines below.

Draw a picture of something that starts with the letter E, such as an elephant or an eagle.

Letter D

Trace the uppercase letter D with your finger.

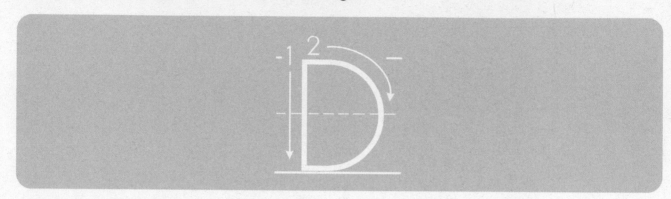

Trace the uppercase letter D with your pencil on the lines below.

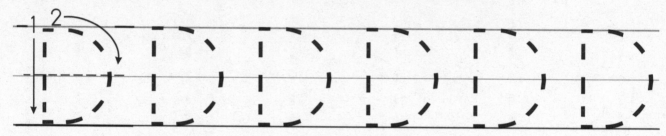

Practice writing the uppercase letter D on the lines below.

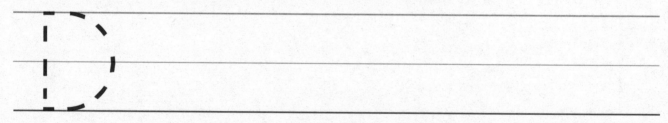

Draw a picture of something that starts with the letter D, such as a dog or a donut.

Letter P

Trace the uppercase letter P with your finger.

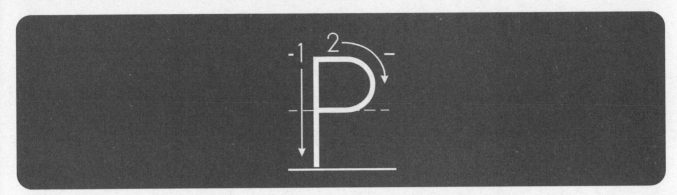

Trace the uppercase letter P with your pencil on the lines below.

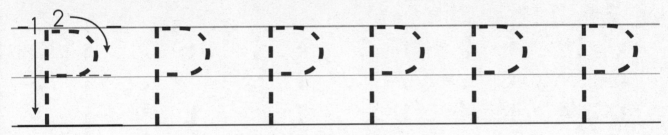

Practice writing the uppercase letter P on the lines below.

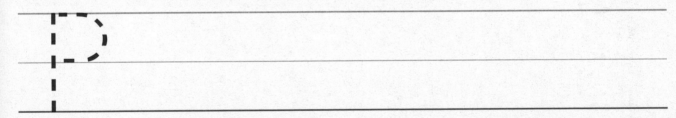

Draw a picture of something that starts with the letter P, such as a pumpkin or a person.

Letter B

Trace the uppercase letter B with your finger.

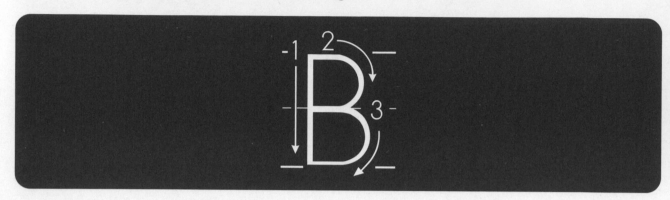

Trace the uppercase letter B with your pencil on the lines below.

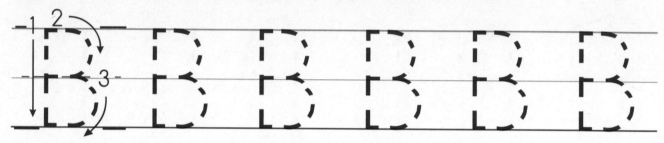

Practice writing the uppercase letter B on the lines below.

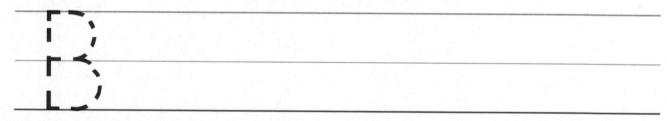

Draw a picture of something that starts with the letter B, such as a boat or a balloon.

Letter R

Trace the uppercase letter R with your finger.

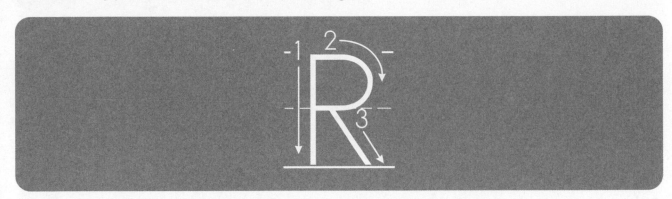

Trace the uppercase letter R with your pencil on the lines below.

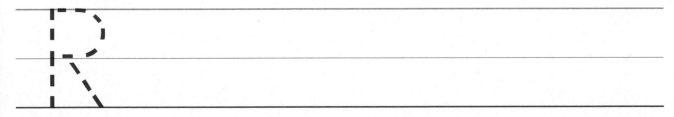

Practice writing the uppercase letter R on the lines below.

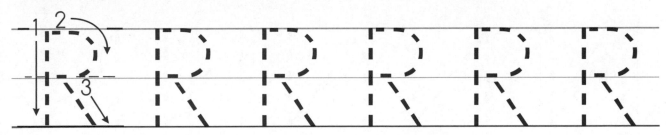

Draw a picture of something that starts with the letter R, such as a rabbit or a rainbow.

Letter N

Trace the uppercase letter N with your finger.

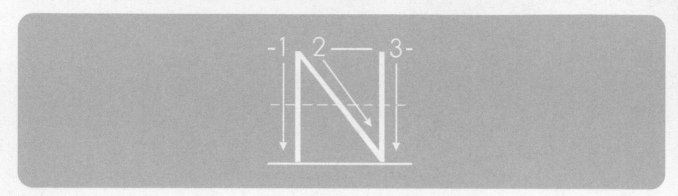

Trace the uppercase letter N with your pencil on the lines below.

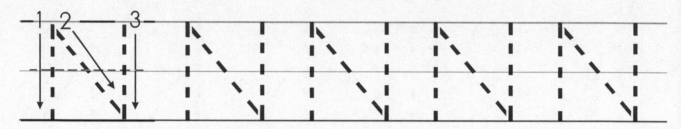

Practice writing the uppercase letter N on the lines below.

Draw a picture of something that starts with the letter N, such as a nest or a net.

Letter M

Trace the uppercase letter M with your finger.

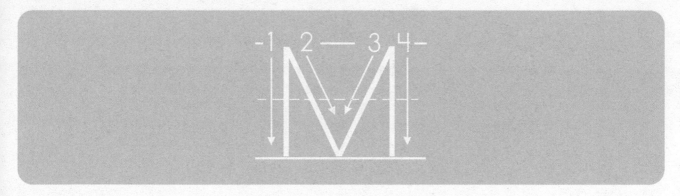

Trace the uppercase letter M with your pencil on the lines below.

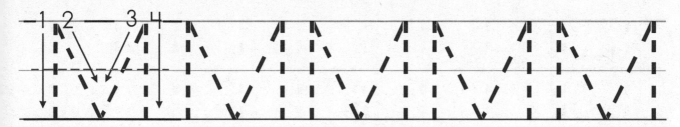

Practice writing the uppercase letter M on the lines below.

Draw a picture of something that starts with the letter M, such as a map or a monkey.

Letter H

Trace the uppercase letter H with your finger.

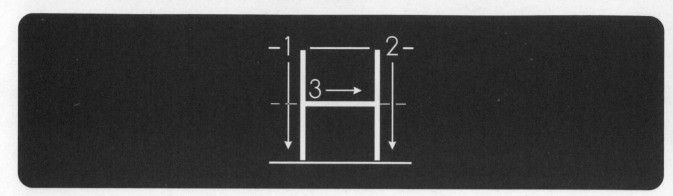

Trace the uppercase letter H with your pencil on the lines below.

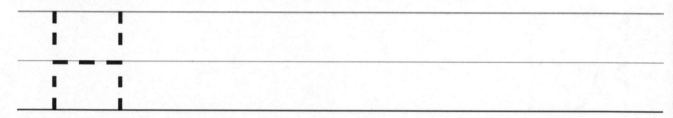

Practice writing the uppercase letter H on the lines below.

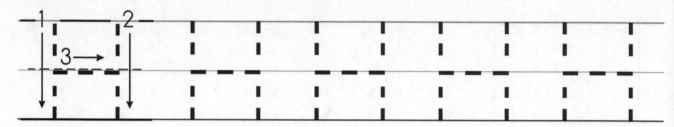

Draw a picture of something that starts with the letter H, such as a house or a hat.

Letter K

Trace the uppercase letter K with your finger.

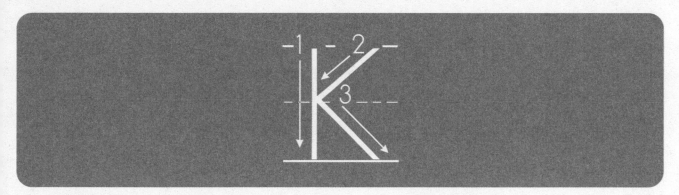

Trace the uppercase letter K with your pencil on the lines below.

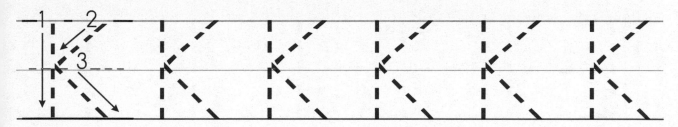

Practice writing the uppercase letter K on the lines below.

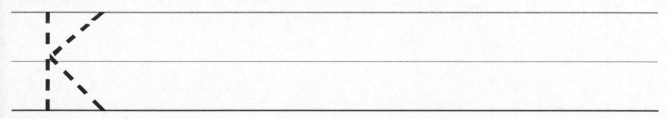

Draw a picture of something that starts with the letter K, such as a kite or a kangaroo.

Letter L

Trace the uppercase letter L with your finger.

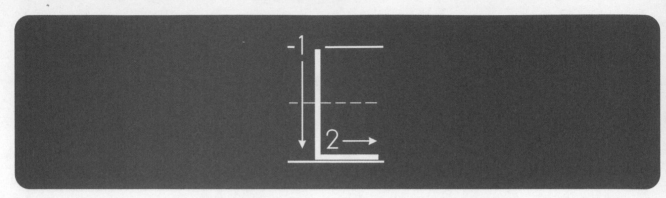

Trace the uppercase letter L with your pencil on the lines below.

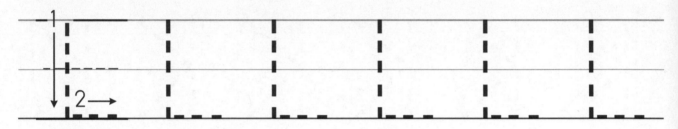

Practice writing the uppercase letter L on the lines below.

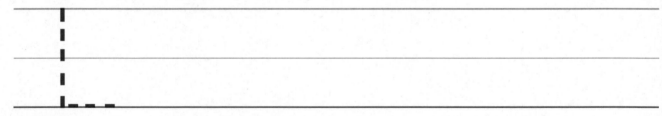

Draw a picture of something that starts with the letter L, such as a lemon or a lion.

Letter U

Trace the uppercase letter U with your finger.

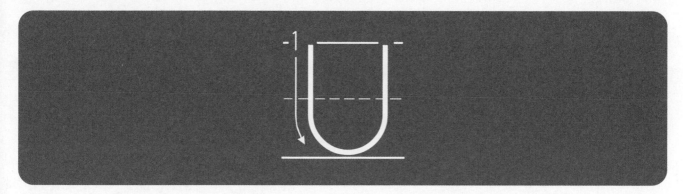

Trace the uppercase letter U with your pencil on the lines below.

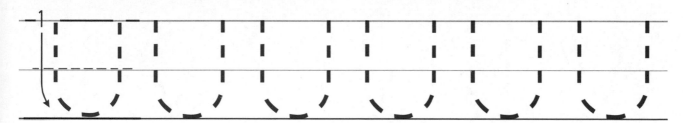

Practice writing the uppercase letter U on the lines below.

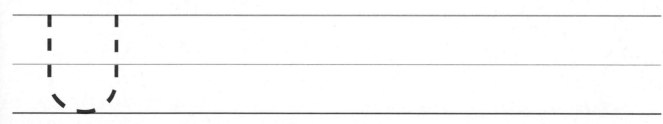

Draw a picture of something that starts with the letter U, such as an umbrella or a unicorn.

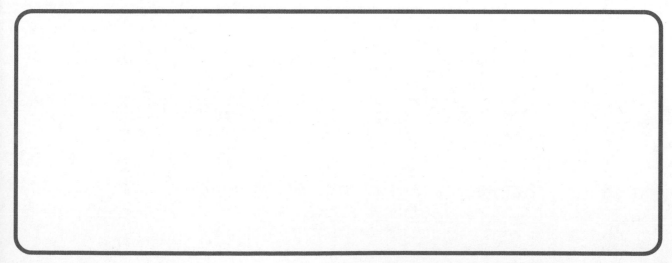

Letter V

Trace the uppercase letter V with your finger.

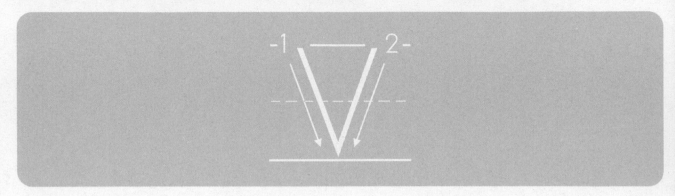

Trace the uppercase letter V with your pencil on the lines below.

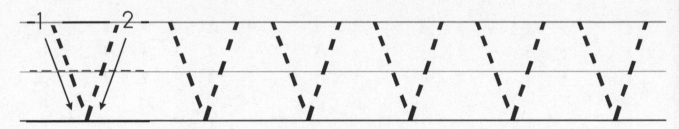

Practice writing the uppercase letter V on the lines below.

Draw a picture of something that starts with the letter V, such as a vase or a van.

Letter W

Trace the uppercase letter W with your finger.

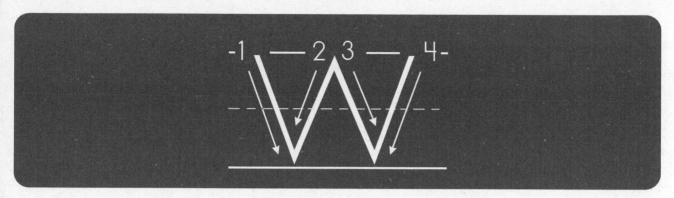

Trace the uppercase letter W with your pencil on the lines below.

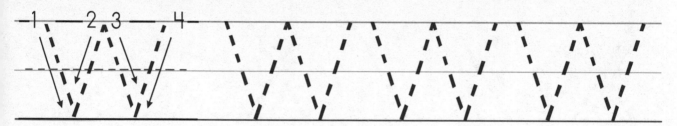

Practice writing the uppercase letter W on the lines below.

Draw a picture of something that starts with the letter W, such as a walrus or a watermelon.

Letter X

Trace the uppercase letter X with your finger.

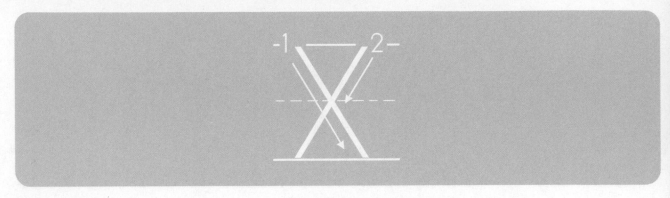

Trace the uppercase letter X with your pencil on the lines below.

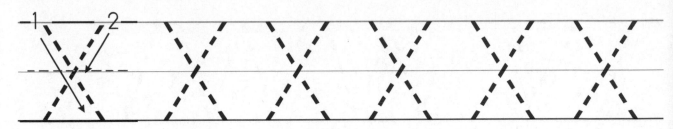

Practice writing the uppercase letter X on the lines below.

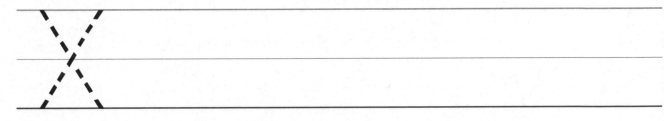

Draw a picture of something that starts with the letter X, such as an x-ray or a xylophone.

Letter Y

Trace the uppercase letter Y with your finger.

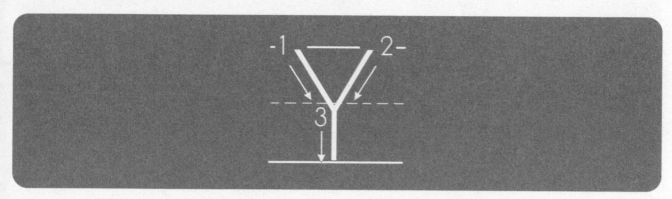

Trace the uppercase letter Y with your pencil on the lines below.

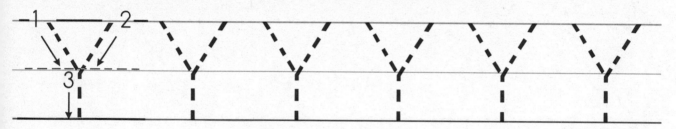

Practice writing the uppercase letter Y on the lines below.

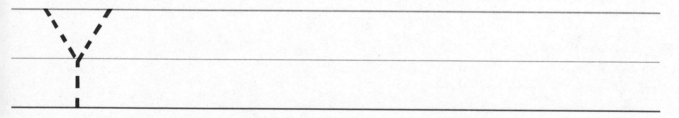

Draw a picture of something that starts with the letter Y, such as a yo-yo or yarn.

Letter Z

Trace the uppercase letter Z with your finger.

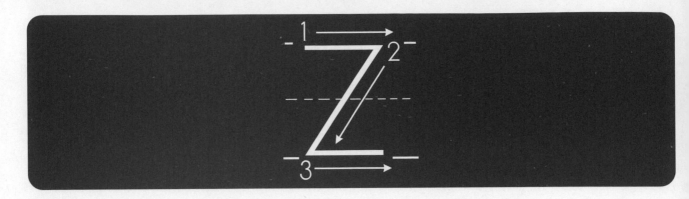

Trace the uppercase letter Z with your pencil on the lines below.

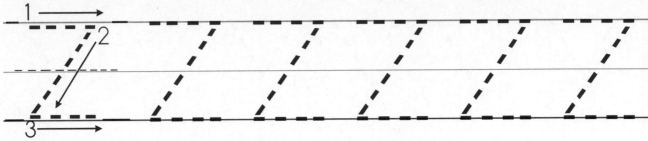

Practice writing the uppercase letter Z on the lines below.

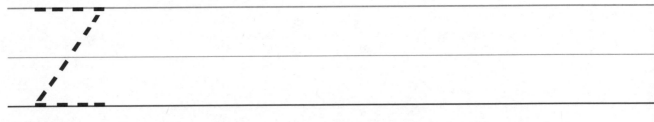

Draw a picture of something that starts with the letter Z, such as a zebra or a zigzag.

Letter C

Trace the uppercase letter C with your finger.

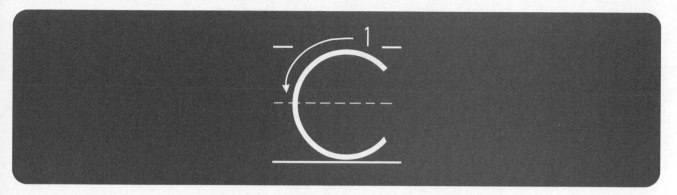

Trace the uppercase letter C with your pencil on the lines below.

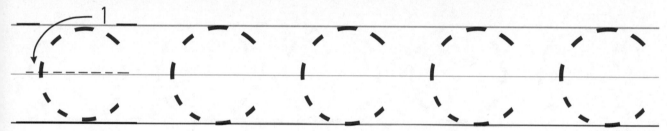

Practice writing the uppercase letter C on the lines below.

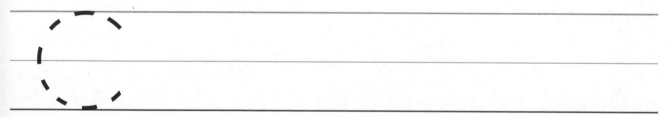

Draw a picture of something that starts with the letter C, such as a cat or a coat.

Letter O

Trace the uppercase letter O with your finger.

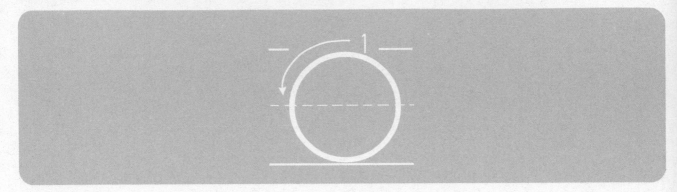

Trace the uppercase letter O with your pencil on the lines below.

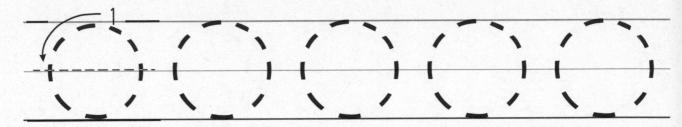

Practice writing the uppercase letter O on the lines below.

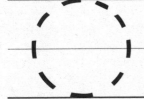

Draw a picture of something that starts with the letter O, such as an owl or an octopus.

Letter Q

Trace the uppercase letter Q with your finger.

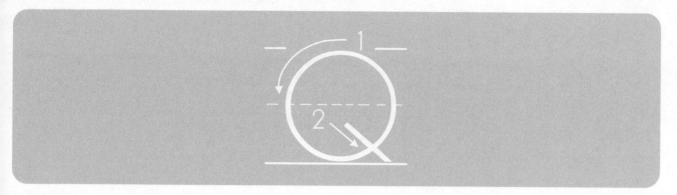

Trace the uppercase letter Q with your pencil on the lines below.

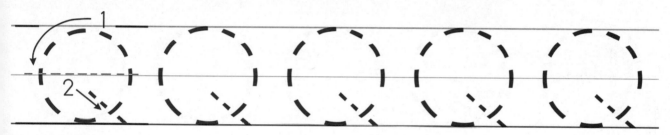

Practice writing the uppercase letter Q on the lines below.

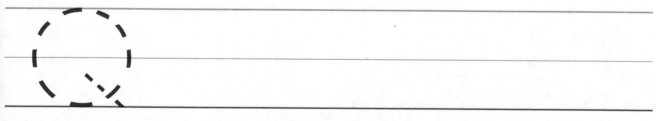

Draw a picture of something that starts with the letter Q, such as a queen or a quilt.

Letter G

Trace the uppercase letter G with your finger.

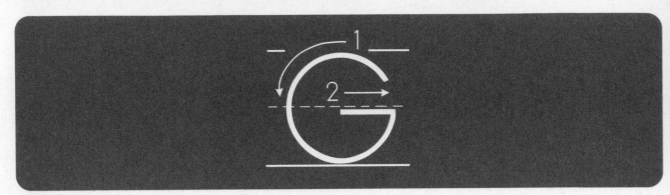

Trace the uppercase letter G with your pencil on the lines below.

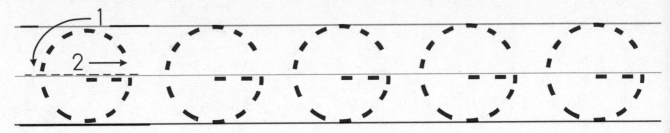

Practice writing the uppercase letter G on the lines below.

Draw a picture of something that starts with the letter G, such as a goose or a goat.

Letter S

Trace the uppercase letter S with your finger.

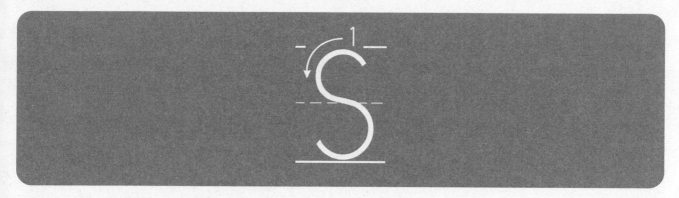

Trace the uppercase letter S with your pencil on the lines below.

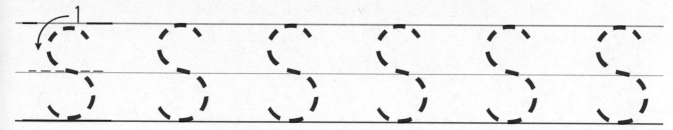

Practice writing the uppercase letter S on the lines below.

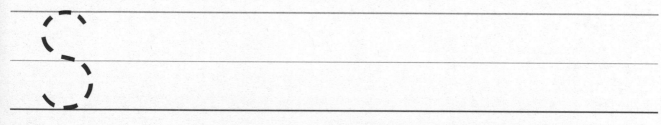

Draw a picture of something that starts with the letter S, such as a snake or a sun.

Letter A

Trace the uppercase letter A with your finger.

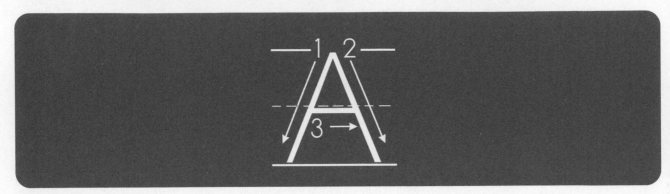

Trace the uppercase letter A with your pencil on the lines below.

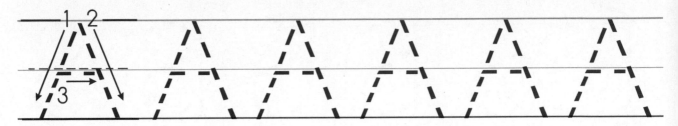

Practice writing the uppercase letter A on the lines below.

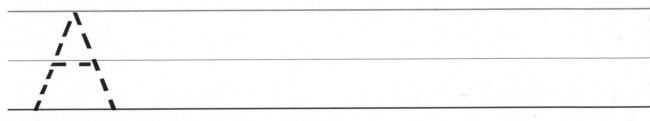

Draw a picture of something that starts with the letter A, such as an acorn or an alligator.

Uppercase Letter Practice

Letter I

Trace the uppercase letter I with your finger.

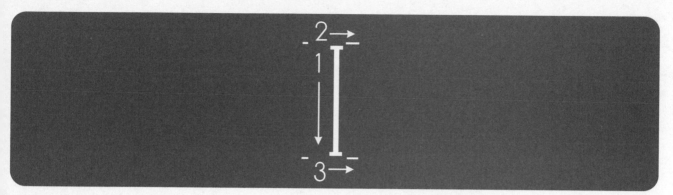

Trace the uppercase letter I with your pencil on the lines below.

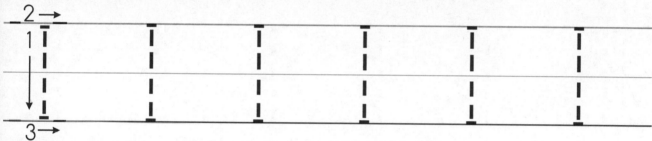

Practice writing the uppercase letter I on the lines below.

Draw a picture of something that starts with the letter I, such as an island or an iguana.

Letter T

Trace the uppercase letter T with your finger.

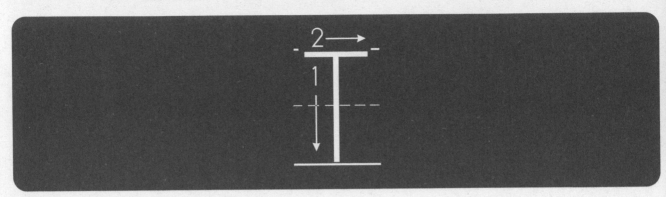

Trace the uppercase letter T with your pencil on the lines below.

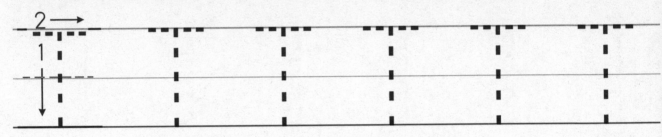

Practice writing the uppercase letter T on the lines below.

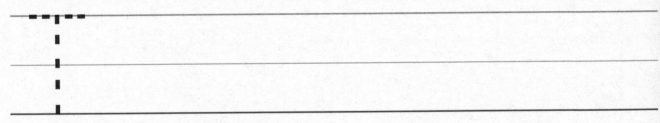

Draw a picture of something that starts with the letter T, such as a tiger or a train.

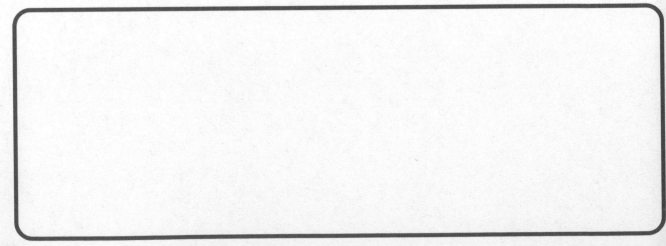

Letter J

Trace the uppercase letter J with your finger.

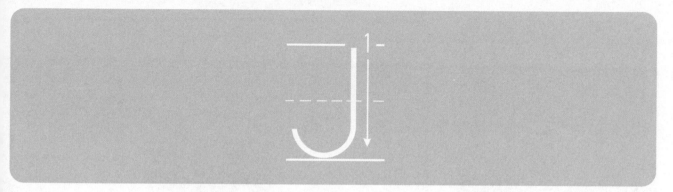

Trace the uppercase letter J with your pencil on the lines below.

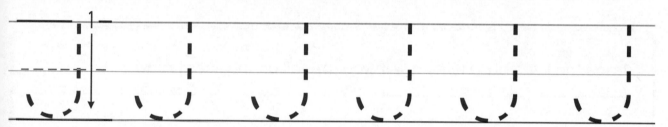

Practice writing the uppercase letter J on the lines below.

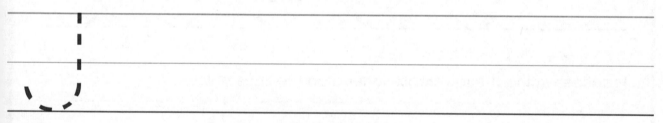

Draw a picture of something that starts with the letter J, such as a jungle or a jacket.

Letter c

Trace the lowercase letter c with your finger.

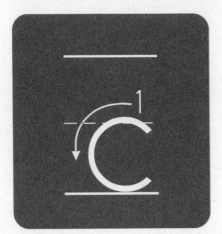

Trace the lowercase letter c with your pencil on the lines below.

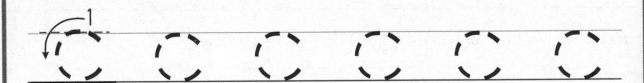

Practice writing the lowercase letter c on the lines below.

Trace the words that start with the letter c on the lines below.

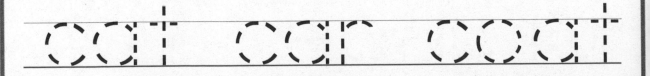

Letter o

Trace the lowercase letter o with your finger.

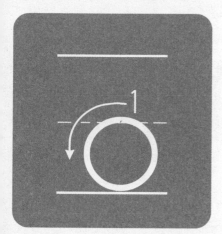

Trace the lowercase letter o with your pencil on the lines below.

Practice writing the lowercase letter o on the lines below.

Trace the words that start with the letter o on the lines below.

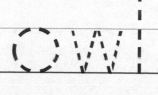

Letter s

Trace the lowercase letter s with your finger.

Trace the lowercase letter s with your pencil on the lines below.

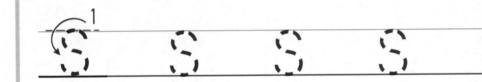

Practice writing the lowercase letter s on the lines below.

Trace the words that start with the letter s on the lines below.

Letter v

Trace the letter v with your finger.

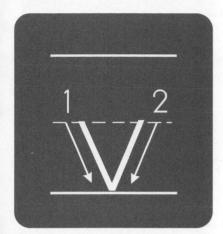

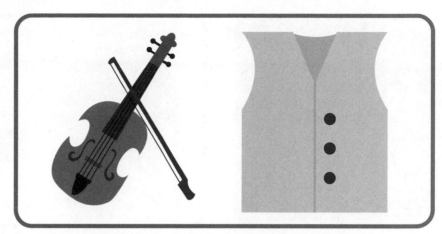

Trace the lowercase letter v with your pencil on the lines below.

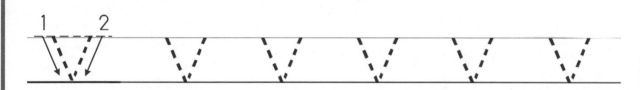

Practice writing the lowercase letter v on the lines below.

Trace the words that start with the lowercase letter v on the lines below.

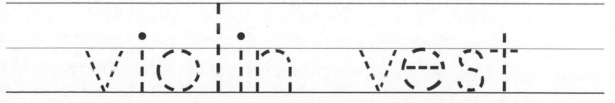

violin vest

Letter w

Trace the lowercase letter w with your finger.

Trace the lowercase letter w with your pencil on the lines below.

Practice writing the lowercase letter w on the lines below.

w

Trace the words that start with the letter w on the lines below.

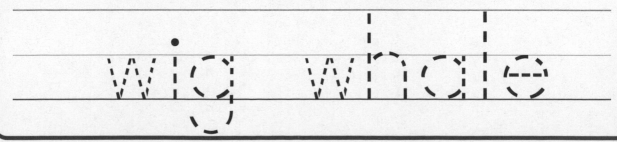

wig whale

Letter t

Trace the lowercase letter t with your finger.

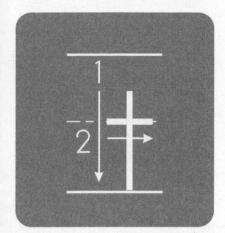

Trace the lowercase letter t with your pencil on the lines below.

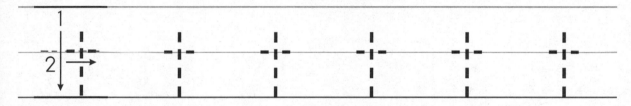

Practice writing the lowercase letter t on the lines below.

Trace the words that start with the letter t on the lines below.

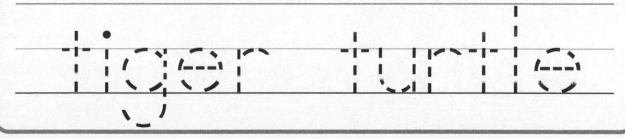

Letter a

Trace the lowercase letter a with your finger.

Trace the lowercase letter a with your pencil on the lines below.

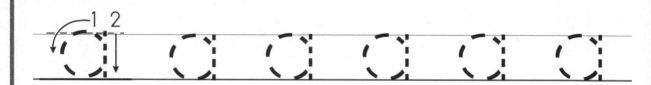

Practice writing the lowercase letter a on the lines below.

Trace the words that start with the letter a on the lines below.

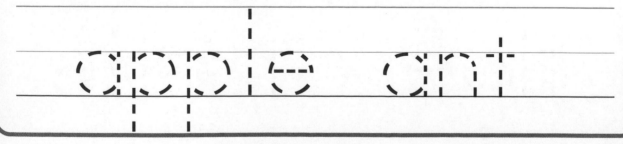

Letter d

Trace the lowercase letter d with your finger.

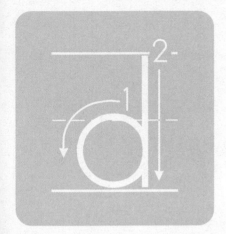

Trace the lowercase letter d with your pencil on the lines below.

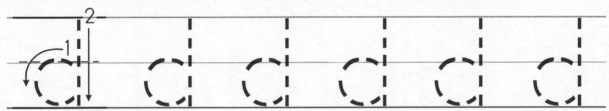

Practice writing the lowercase letter d on the lines below.

Trace the words that start with the letter d on the lines below.

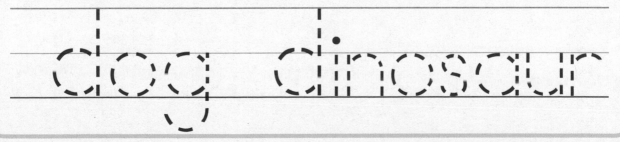

Letter g

Trace the lowercase letter g with your finger.

Trace the lowercase letter g with your pencil on the lines below.

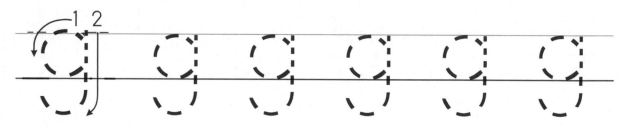

Practice writing the lowercase letter g on the lines below.

Trace the words that start with the letter g on the lines below.

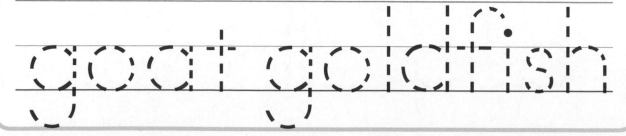

Letter u

Trace the lowercase letter u with your finger.

Trace the lowercase letter u with your pencil on the lines below.

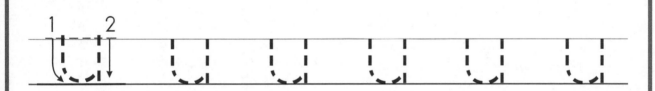

Practice writing the lowercase letter u on the lines below.

Trace the words that start with the letter u on the lines below.

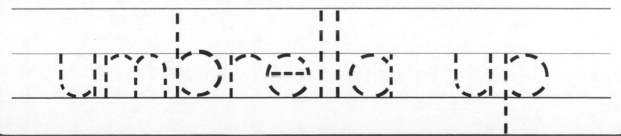

Letter i

Trace the lowercase letter i with your finger.

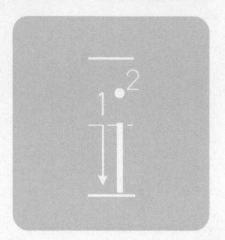 

Trace the lowercase letter i with your pencil on the lines below.

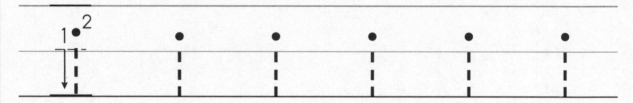

Practice writing the lowercase letter i on the lines below.

Trace the words that start with the letter i on the lines below.

Letter e

Trace the lowercase letter e with your finger.

Trace the lowercase letter e with your pencil on the lines below.

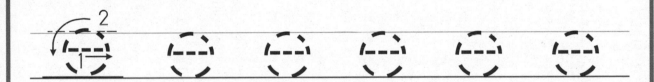

Practice writing the lowercase letter e on the lines below.

Trace the words that start with the letter e on the lines below.

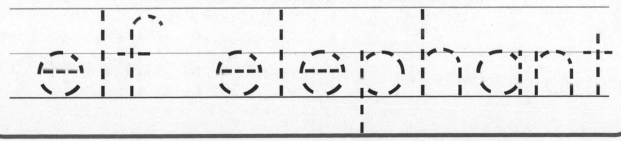

Letter l

Trace the lowercase letter l with your finger.

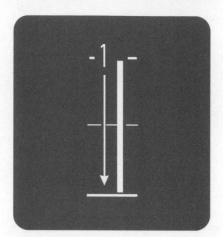

Trace the lowercase letter l with your pencil on the lines below.

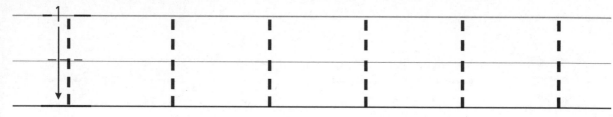

Practice writing the lowercase letter l on the lines below.

Trace the words that start with the letter l on the lines below.

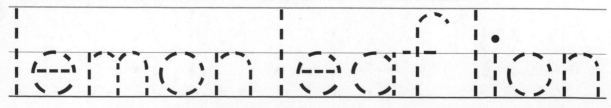

Letter k

Trace the lowercase letter k with your finger.

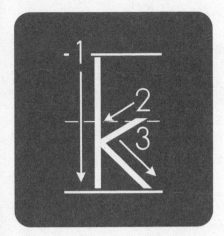

Trace the lowercase letter k with your pencil on the lines below.

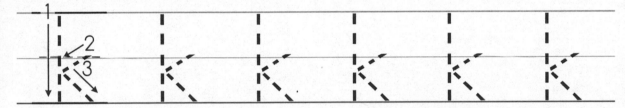

Practice writing the lowercase letter k on the lines below.

Trace the words that start with the letter k on the lines below.

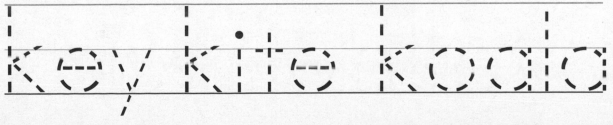

Letter y

Trace the lowercase letter y with your finger.

Trace the lowercase letter y with your pencil on the lines below.

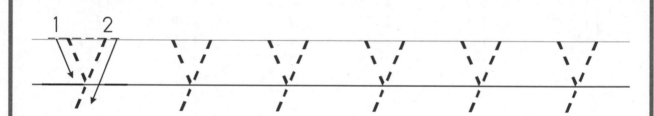

Practice writing the lowercase letter y on the lines below.

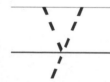

Trace the words that start with the letter y on the lines below.

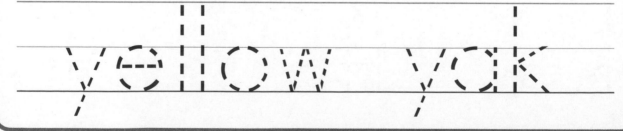

Lowercase Letter Practice

Letter j

Trace the lowercase letter j with your finger.

Trace the lowercase letter j with your pencil on the lines below.

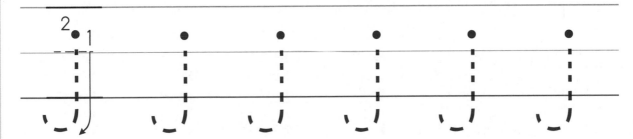

Practice writing the lowercase letter j on the lines below.

Trace the words that start with the letter j on the lines below.

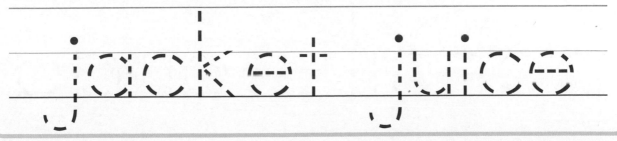

Letter p

Trace the lowercase letter p with your finger.

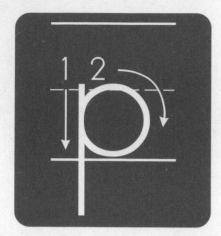

Trace the lowercase letter p with your pencil on the lines below.

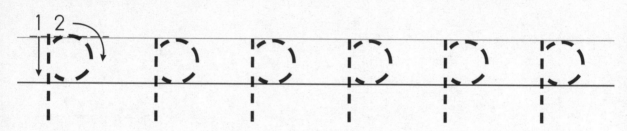

Practice writing the lowercase letter p on the lines below.

Trace the words that start with the letter p on the lines below.

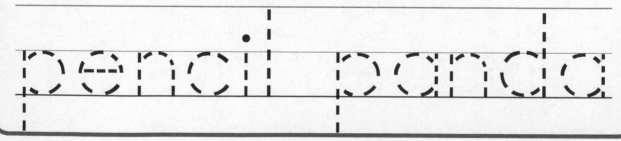

pencil panda

Lowercase Letter Practice

Letter r

Trace the lowercase letter r with your finger.

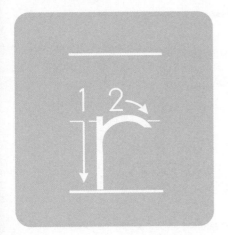 

Trace the lowercase letter r with your pencil on the lines below.

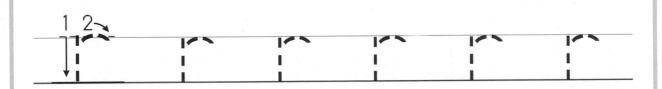

Practice writing the lowercase letter r on the lines below.

Trace the words that start with the letter r on the lines below.

rooster rabbit

Letter n

Trace the lowercase letter n with your finger.

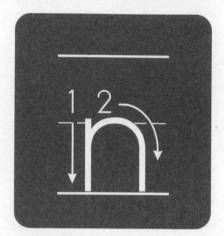

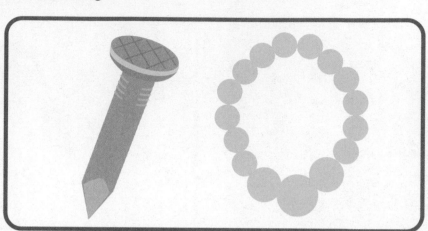

Trace the lowercase letter n with your pencil on the lines below.

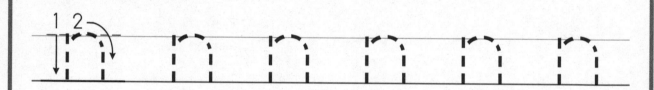

Practice writing the lowercase letter n on the lines below.

Trace the words that start with the letter n on the lines below.

nail necklace

Letter m

Trace the lowercase letter m with your finger.

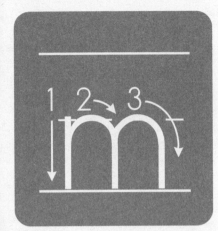

Trace the lowercase letter m with your pencil on the lines below.

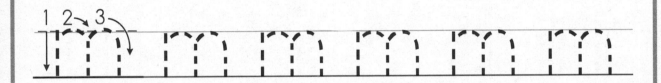

Practice writing the lowercase letter m on the lines below.

Trace the words that start with the letter m on the lines below.

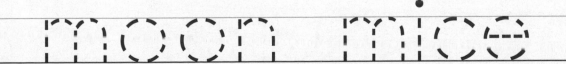

113

Letter h

Trace the lowercase letter h with your finger.

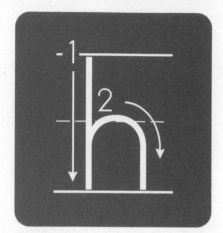

Trace the lowercase letter h with your pencil on the lines below.

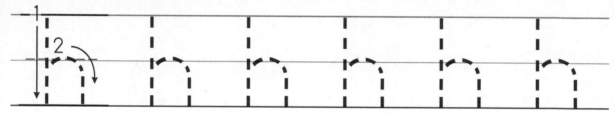

Practice writing the lowercase letter h on the lines below.

Trace the words that start with the letter h on the lines below.

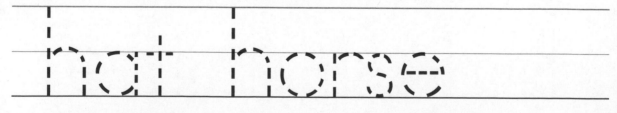

Letter b

Trace the lowercase letter b with your finger.

Trace the lowercase letter b with your pencil on the lines below.

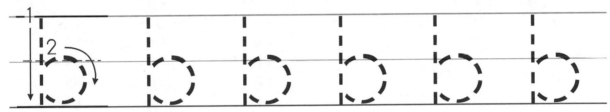

Practice writing the lowercase letter b on the lines below.

Trace the words that start with the letter b on the lines below.

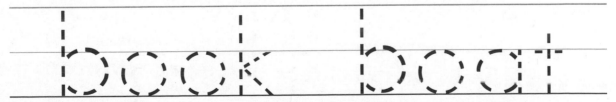

Letter f

Trace the lowercase letter f with your finger.

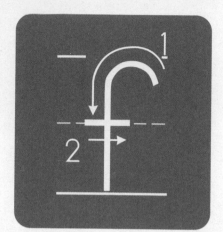

Trace the lowercase letter f with your pencil on the lines below.

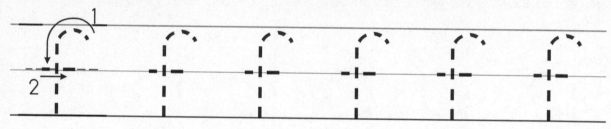

Practice writing the lowercase letter f on the lines below.

Trace the words that start with the letter f on the lines below.

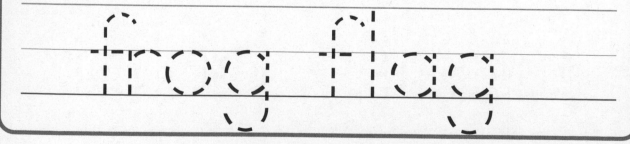

Letter q

Trace the lowercase letter q with your finger.

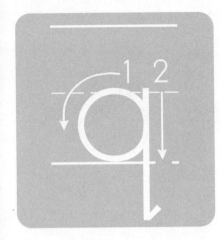

Trace the lowercase letter q with your pencil on the lines below.

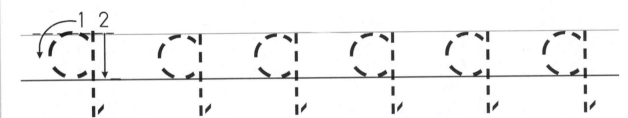

Practice writing the lowercase letter q on the lines below.

Trace the words that start with the letter q on the lines below.

Letter x

Trace the lowercase letter x with your finger.

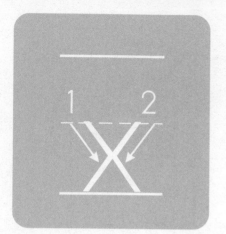

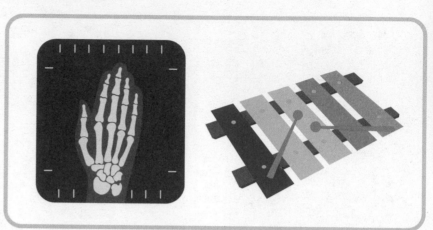

Trace the lowercase letter x with your pencil on the lines below.

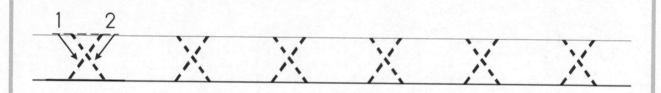

Practice writing the lowercase letter x on the lines below.

Trace the words that start with the letter x on the lines below.

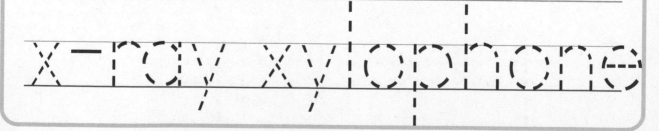

Letter z

Trace the lowercase letter z with your finger.

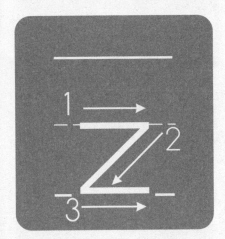
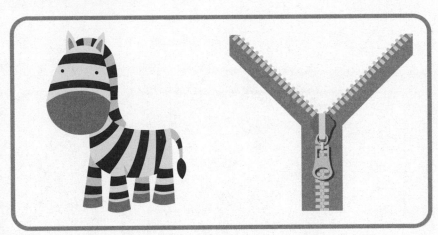

Trace the lowercase letter z with your pencil on the lines below.

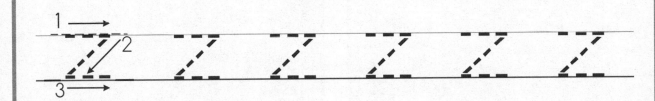

Practice writing the lowercase letter z on the lines below.

Trace the words that start with the letter z on the lines below.

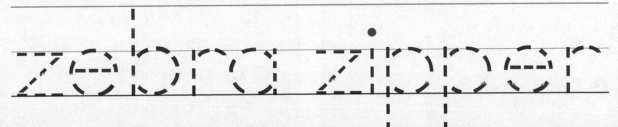

Using your favorite crayon, draw a line from the uppercase letter to the matching lowercase letter.

B	h	A	o
Q	g	E	l
G	j	K	a
H	b	C	n
J	d	L	c
S	q	N	t
Y	s	P	e
D	y	R	k
F	m	T	p
M	f	O	r

Sight Words

Read and trace the sight words below.

Choose your favorite crayons. Then read the words and trace each letter in a different color.

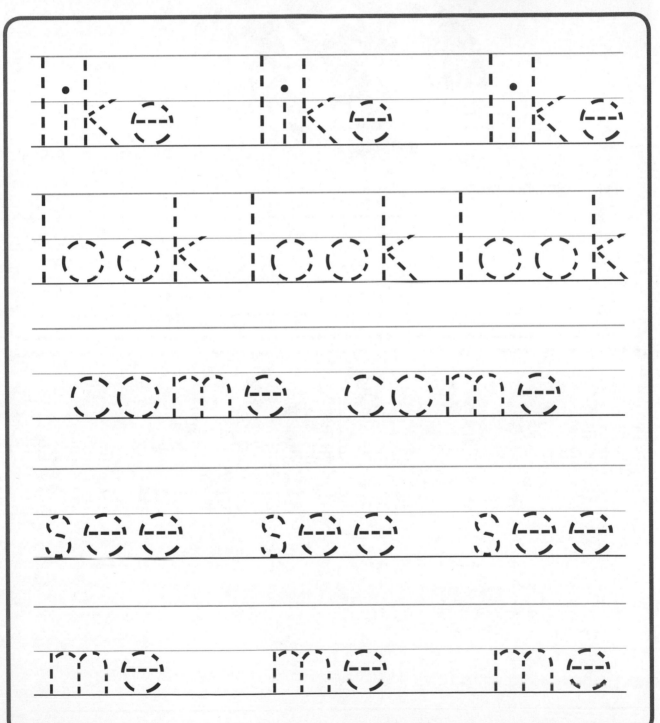

Let's Write Sentences!

Look at the pictures and read the sentences. Write another sentence about the pictures on the lines below.

I like to play hockey.

_____

_____

_____

I like camping.

_____

_____

_____

Writing Sentences

Let's Write Sentences!

Look at the pictures and read the sentences. Write another sentence about the pictures on the lines below.

I like pancakes.

_____

_____

We play catch.

_____

_____

Making a List

Make a list of ten of your favorite foods. Write one item on each line to make a list.

1.

2.

3.

4.

5.

6.

7.

8.

9.

10.

Brainstorming Writing Topics

Draw a picture of your family in the box.

Write about your family on the lines below.

_____

_____

_____

_____

_____

_____

_____

_____

CERTIFICATE
of Achievement

....

has successfully completed **Kindergarten Writing**

Date: ....

Signed: ....

1²3 Math

Table of Contents

Research shows that certain kinds of parent-child interactions in a child's early years, commonly referred to as "number talk," can be a primary driver of mathematical ability through fifth grade. Follow the directions for the games and activities throughout this book and watch your child's mathematical abilities grow!

Vocabulary Builder

Understanding Numbers Game

Make your way from the car to the campground by following the path of numbers 1-20 in the correct order. Make sure to point to each number as you say it!

Trace the number 1 and the word one with your finger. Then practice writing the number and the word on the lines below.

one

one one one

one

Count the insects and write the number 1 and the word one on the lines below.

Trace the number 2 and the word two with your finger. Then practice writing the number and the word on the lines below.

Practice writing the number 2 on the lines below.

Circle the set of two apples below.

Trace the number 3 and the word three with your finger. Then practice writing the number and the word on the lines below.

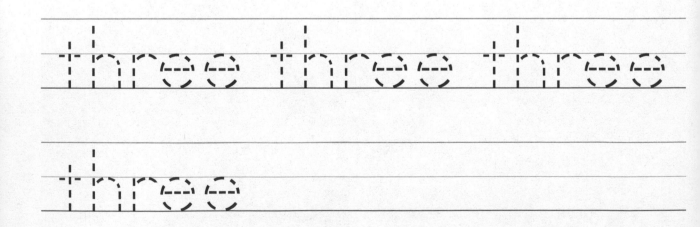

Circle each set of three dogs. Practice writing the number 3 on the lines below.

Trace the number 4 and the word four with your finger. Then practice writing the number and the word on the lines below.

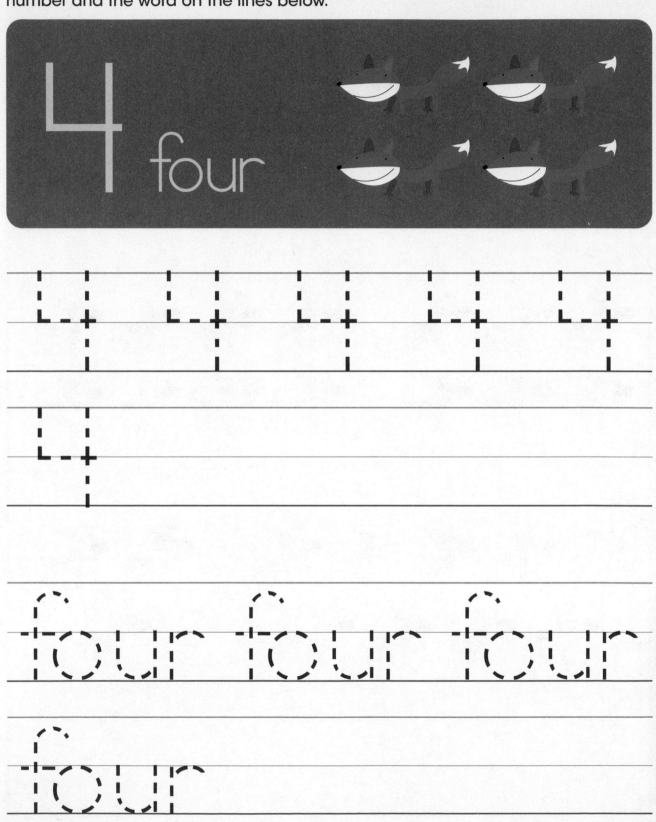

Where are the chocolate chips? Draw four chocolate chips on the cookie. Practice writing the number 4 on the lines below.

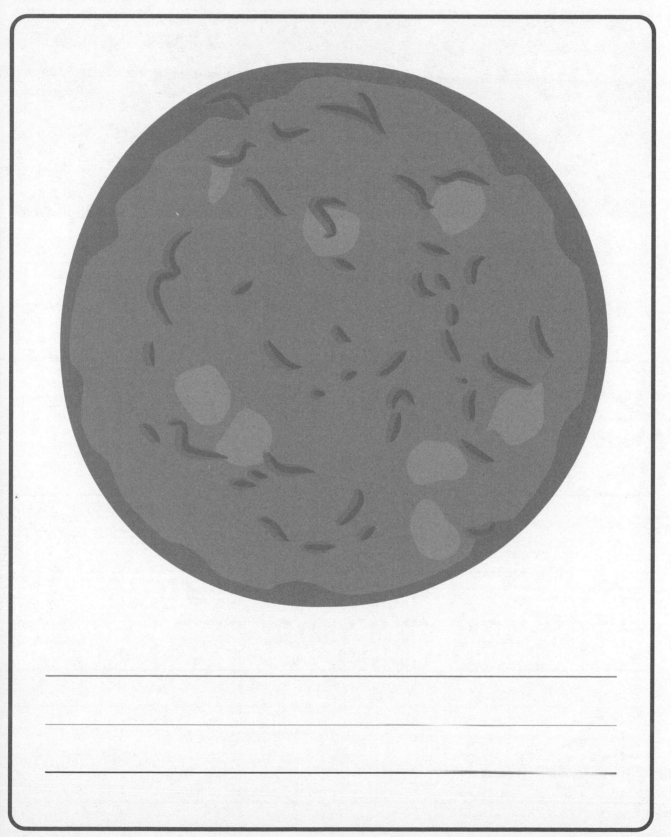

Trace the number 5 and the word five with your finger. Then practice writing the number and the word on the lines below.

Understanding Numbers 1–5

How many swans are in the pond? Count the swans. Then color the swans and write the number on the lines below.

Count the objects and write the number and the word on the lines below.

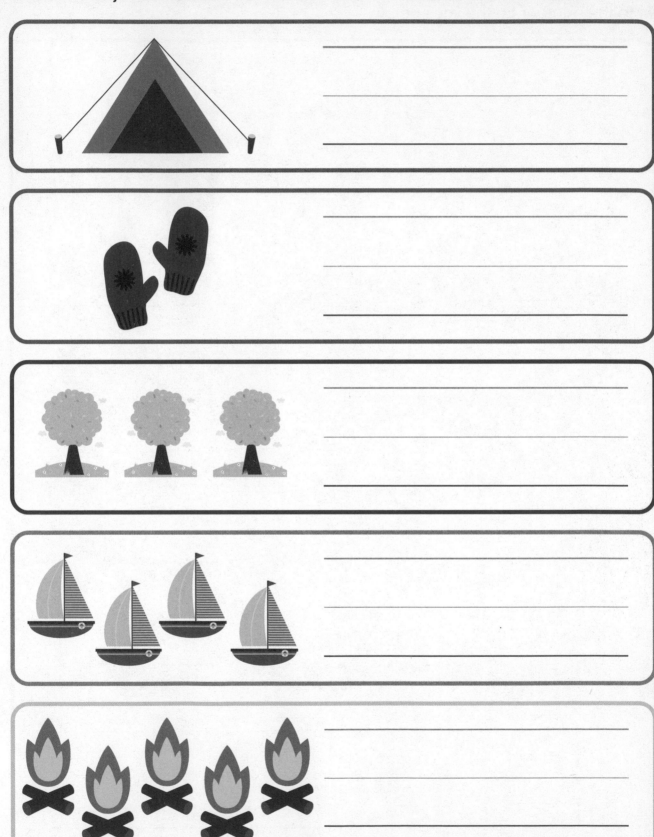

Trace the numbers below. Then draw a line from the number to the matching set of objects.

Trace the number 6 and the word six with your finger. Then practice writing the number and the word on the lines below.

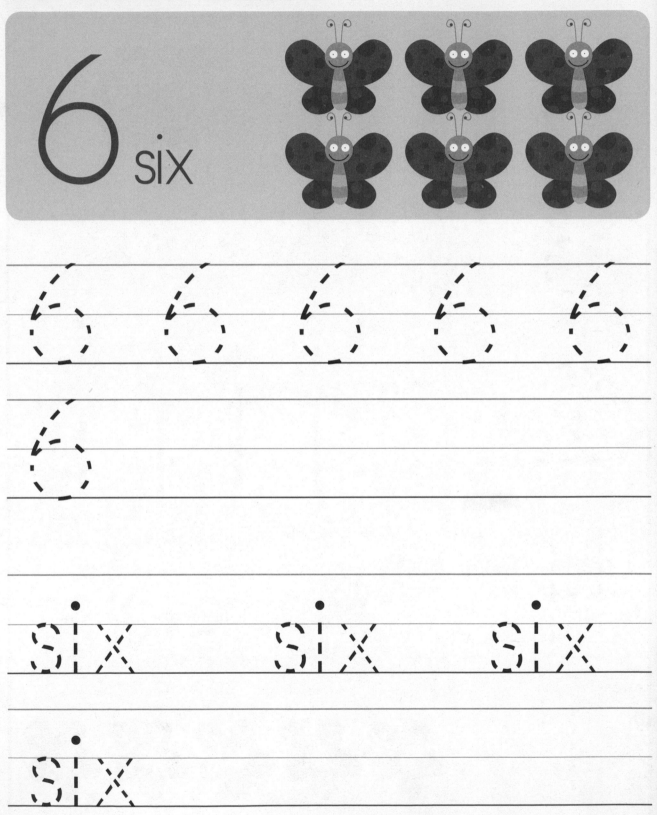

Count the animals and write the number on the lines below.

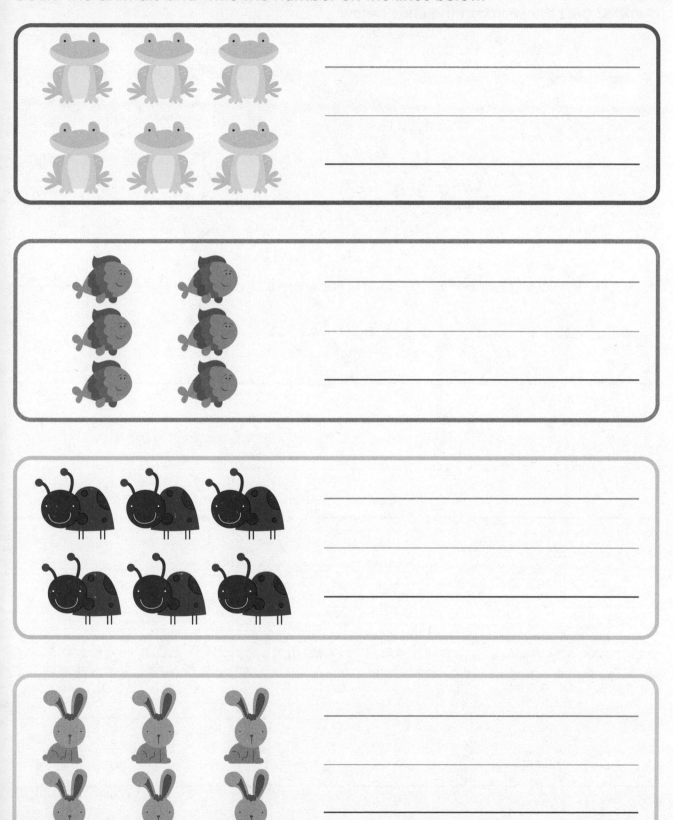

Trace the number 7 and the word seven with your finger. Then practice writing the number and the word on the lines below.

7 seven

7 7 7 7 7

7

seven seven seven

seven

Practice writing the number 7 on the lines below.

Circle each set of seven fruits below.

Trace the number 8 and the word eight with your finger. Then practice writing the number and the word on the lines below.

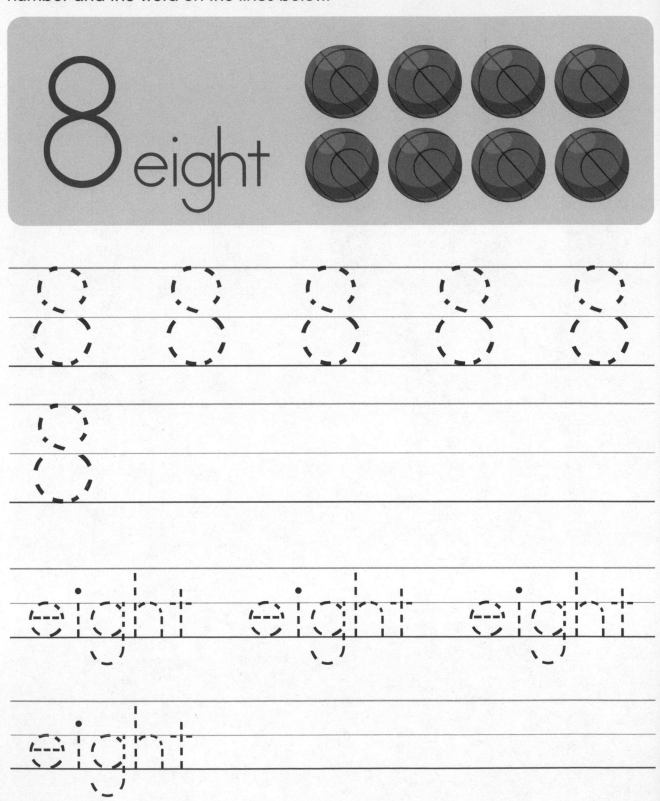

8 eight

Circle each set of eight cats. Practice writing the number 8 on the lines below.

Trace the number 9 and the word nine with your finger. Then practice writing the number and word on the lines below.

Understanding Numbers 6–10

Where are the balloons? Draw nine balloons on top of the strings. Practice writing the number 9 on the lines below.

Trace the number 10 and the word ten with your finger. Then practice writing the number and the word on the lines below.

How many leaves are on the tree? Count the leaves. Then color the leaves and write the number on the lines below.

Count the vehicles and write the number on the lines below.

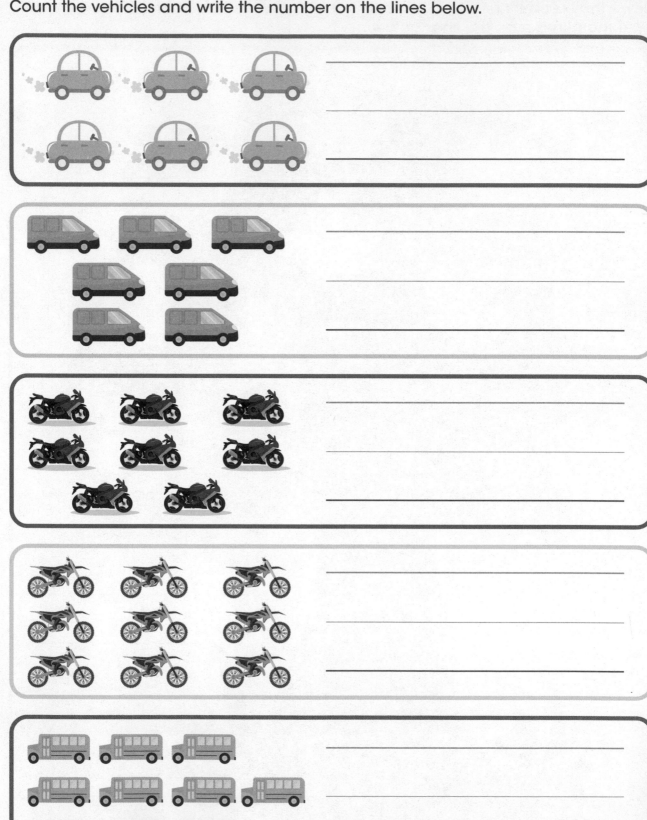

Counting Numbers 6–10

Trace the numbers below. Then draw a line from the number to the matching set of objects.

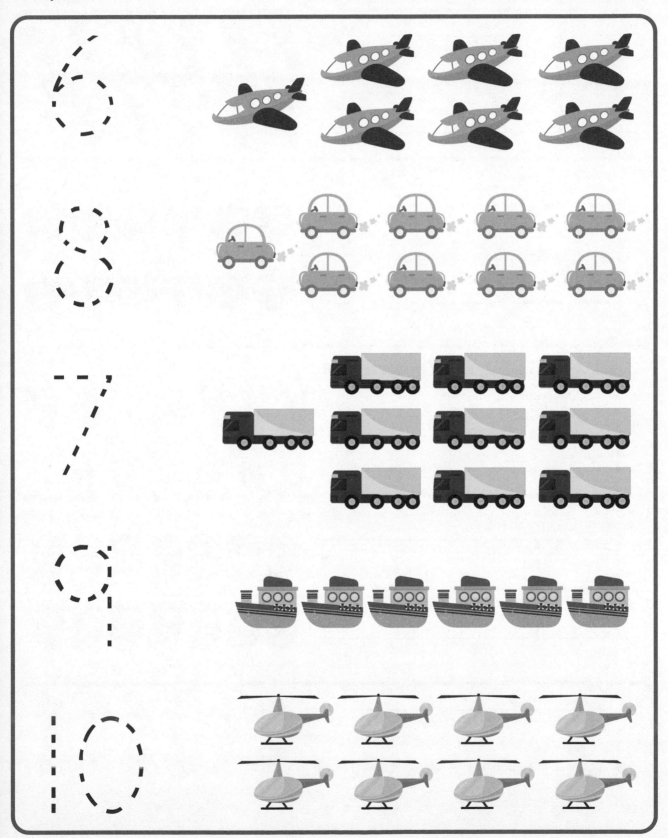

Count the pictures. Then trace the numbers with your finger and practice writing the numbers with a pencil on the lines below.

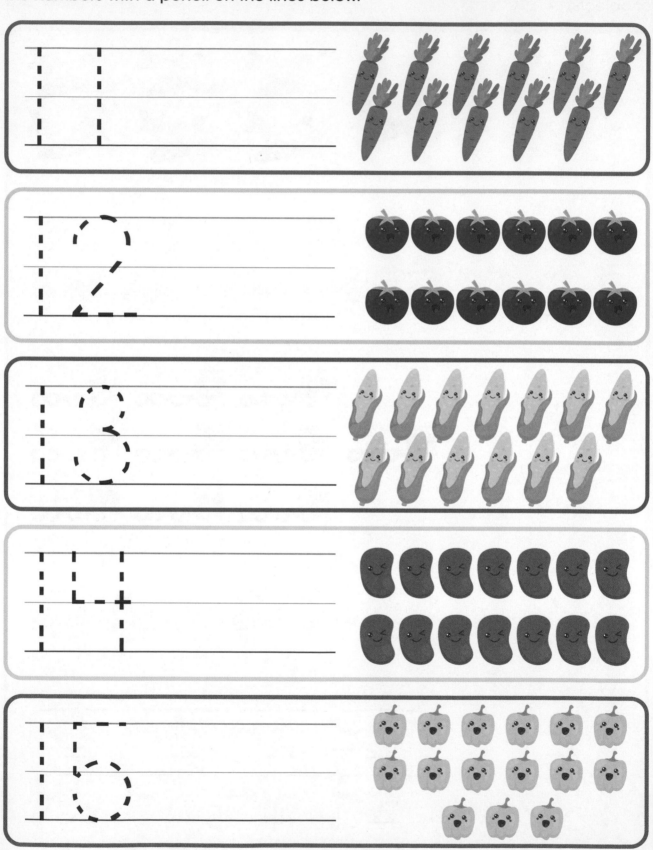

Understanding Numbers 11–20

Count the objects and circle the correct number below each set of pictures.

11   12   13   14   15

11   12   13   14   15

11   12   13   14   15

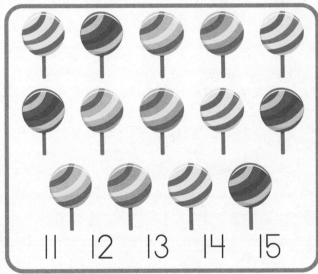

11   12   13   14   15

11   12   13   14   15

Count the pictures. Then trace the numbers with your finger and practice writing the numbers with a pencil on the lines below.

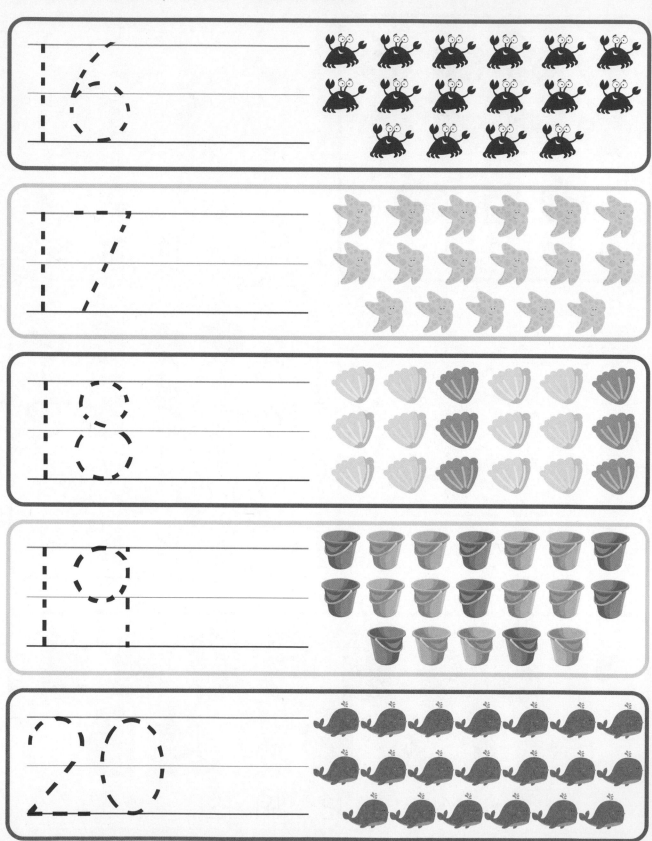

Count the objects and circle the correct number below each set of pictures.

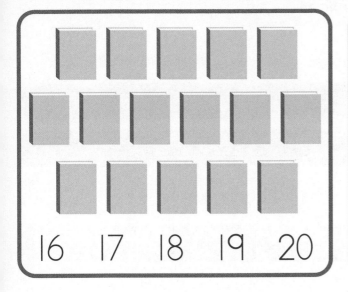

16   17   18   19   20

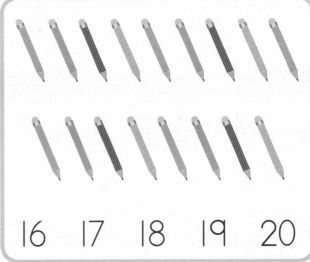

16   17   18   19   20

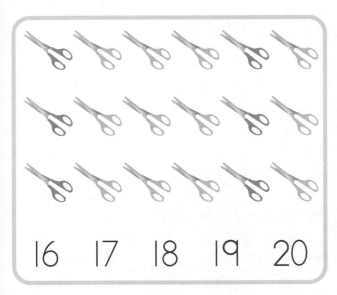

16   17   18   19   20

16   17   18   19   20

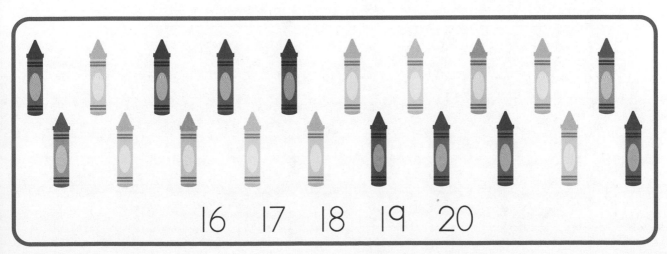

16   17   18   19   20

Adding Numbers 1–10

Adding and subtracting are skills that your child can learn using pictures or real objects. Singing songs is another great way to learn these skills! Try singing "Five Little Monkeys Jumping on a Bed" to practice!

Vocabulary Builder

add	putting two numbers together
in all	the total amount of the numbers put together
subtract	taking away a number from an amount
are left	the amount you have after taking a number away

Point to and count the kids who are swinging. Write the number on the lines below. Count how many kids are jumping rope and write the number on the lines below. How many kids are playing in all? Write the number on the lines below.

How many kids
are swinging?

2

How many kids
are jumping rope?

1

How many kids
are playing in all?

3

Point to and count the red dots. Write the number on the lines below. Count the blue dots and write the number on the lines below. How many red and blue dots are there in all? Write the number on the lines below.

How many red dots are there?

How many blue dots are there?

How many red and blue dots are there in all?

Adding Numbers 1–10

Point to and count the seashells on the beach. Write the number on the lines below. Count how many sandcastles there are and write the number on the lines below. How many seashells and sandcastles are there in all? Write the number on the lines below.

How many seashells are there?

_____

_____

_____

How many sandcastles are there?

_____

_____

_____

How many seashells and sandcastles are there in all?

_____

_____

Adding Numbers 1–10

Point to and count the green blocks you see. Write the number on the lines below. Count how many yellow blocks there are and write the number on the lines below. How many green and yellow blocks are there in all? Write the number on the lines below.

How many green blocks are there?

_____

_____

_____

How many yellow blocks are there?

_____

_____

_____

How many green and yellow blocks are there in all?

_____

_____

Point to and count the frogs you can see. Write the number on the lines below. Count how many lily pads there are and write the number on the lines below. How many frogs and lily pads are there in all? Write the number on the lines below.

How many frogs
are there?
_____

_____

_____

How many lily pads
are there?
_____

_____

_____

How many frogs
and lily pads
are there in all?   _____

Point to and count all of the cats in the picture. Write the number on the lines below. Cross out the gray cats. How many gray cats did you cross out? How many cats are left? Write the numbers on the lines below.

How many cats
are there in all?

_____

_____

_____

How many cats
are left?

_____

How many gray cats
did you cross out?

_____

_____

_____

_____

Point to and count all of the cubes below. Write the number on the lines below. Cross out the blue cubes. How many blue cubes did you cross out? How many cubes are left? Write the numbers on the lines below.

How many cubes
are there in all?

_____

_____

_____

How many blue cubes
did you cross out?

_____

_____

_____

How many cubes
are left?   _____

Point to and count all of the deer in the picture. Write the number on the lines below. Cross out the deer without spots. How many deer without spots did you cross out? How many deer are left? Write the numbers on the lines below.

How many deer
are there in all?

_____

_____

_____

How many deer without
spots did you cross out?

_____

_____

_____

_____

How many deer
are left?   _____

Subtracting Numbers 1–10

Point to and count all of the circles. Write the number on the lines below. Cross out the yellow circles. How many yellow circles did you cross out? How many circles are left? Write the numbers on the lines below.

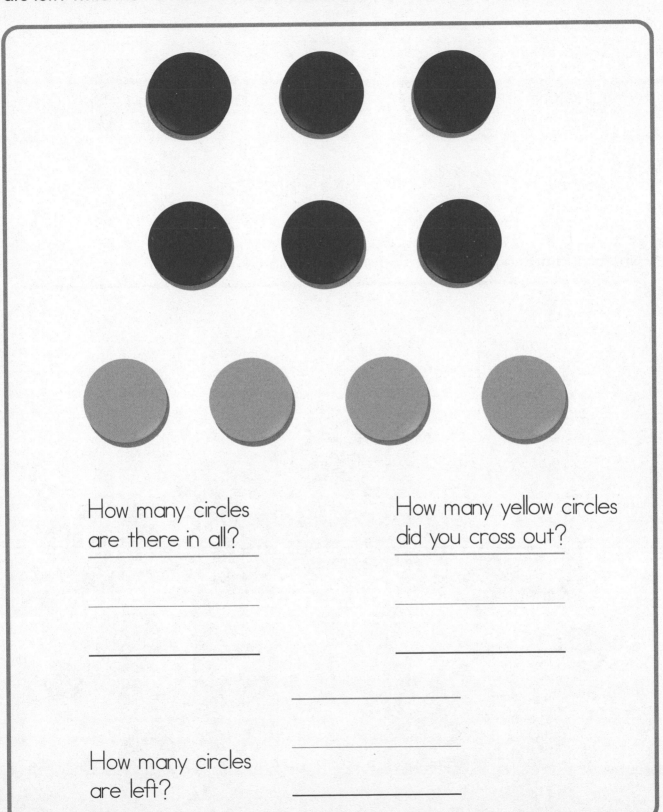

How many circles are there in all?
_____

_____

How many yellow circles did you cross out?
_____

_____

How many circles are left? _____

Shapes

Knowing the primary shapes is the foundation for building knowledge of two-dimensional and three-dimensional geometric figures. Help your child by tracing, drawing, and naming the shapes together.

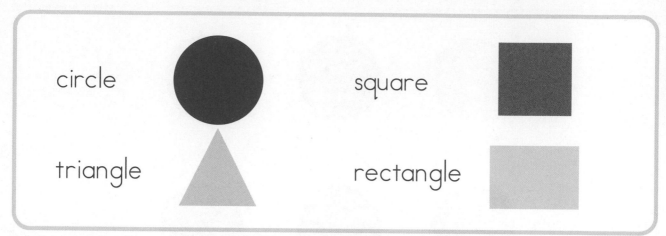

circle

square

triangle

rectangle

Point to and name the shapes you see in the picture below.

Shapes

Name That Shape!

Circle the correct name of the shapes below.

circle   square

triangle   rectangle

circle   square

triangle   rectangle

circle   square

triangle   rectangle

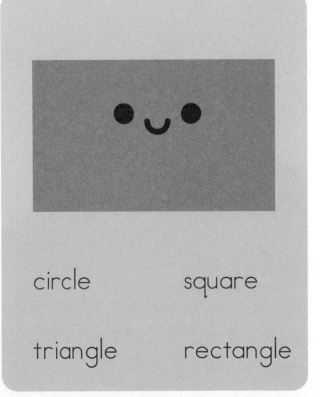

circle   square

triangle   rectangle

Shapes

Count the shapes in the picture. Write the number of each shape on the lines below. Then color the shapes.

_____

_____

_____ circles

_____

_____

_____ rectangles

_____

_____

_____ squares

_____

_____

_____ triangle

Shapes

Shape Jumble!

Color Key

Circle:	Red	Square:	Green
Rectangle:	Blue	Triangle:	Orange

Color the shapes below using the color key.

Understanding Measurement

We measure things in many ways every day. Conversations about how long it is until lunchtime, how far it is to the park, and how tall your child is getting will engage your child in the process of learning these skills. Before you know it, they will be telling time, measuring, and comparing sizes of objects!

Longer and Shorter

Circle the objects that are longer. Cross out the objects that are shorter.

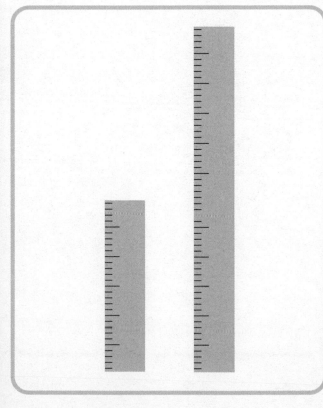

Bigger and Smaller

Circle the objects that are bigger. Cross out the objects that are smaller.

Understanding Measurement

Heavier and Lighter

Circle the objects that are heavier. Cross out the objects that are lighter.

Understanding Time

What time is it? Some things happen during the day and some things happen at night. Draw a line from the time of day to the matching picture.

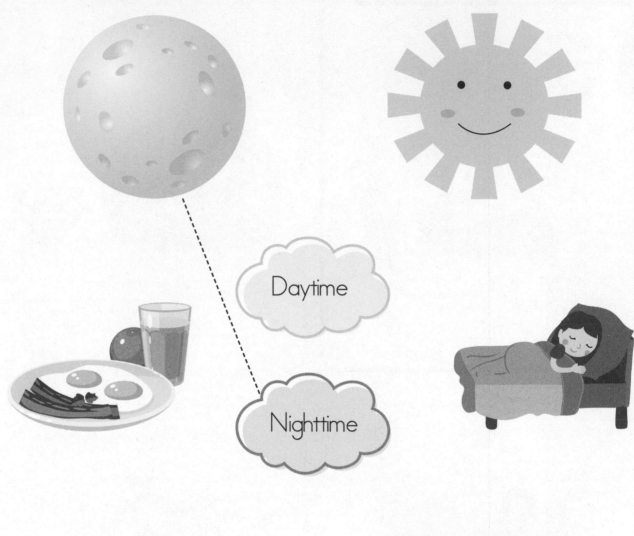

Daytime

Nighttime

Let's Talk About a Clock!

A clock has numbers from 1 to 12 on its face. Complete the picture of the clock by writing the missing numbers in the circles.

Sorting and Categorizing

Naturally, when children explore everything around them, they notice how things are alike and how things are different. Sorting and categorizing are best learned when they are part of a child's everyday life. Common activities that children experience during play and daily tasks they perform provide many opportunities for them to learn these math concepts.

Same

Circle the objects that are the same in each row.

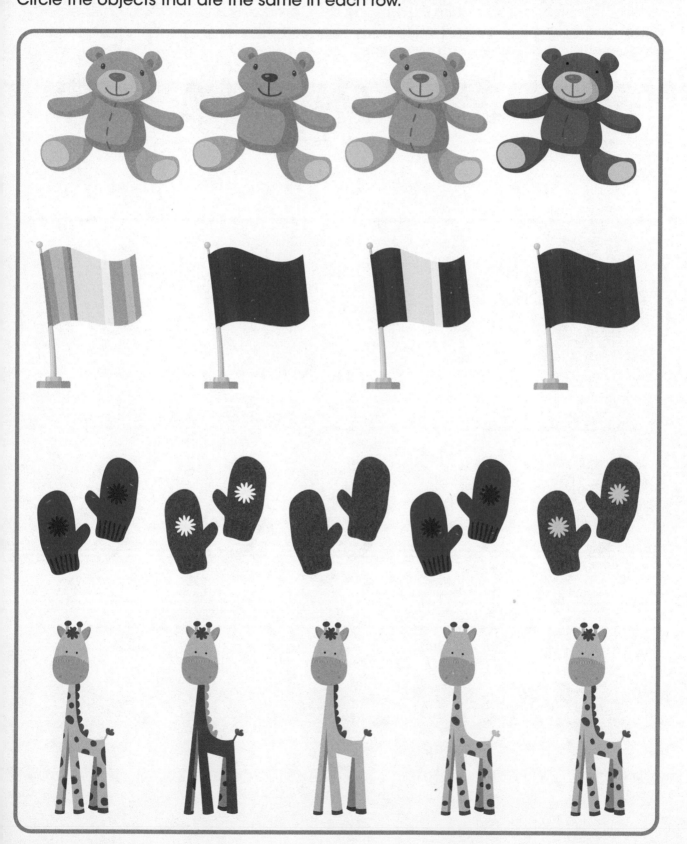

Different

Cross out the objects that are different in each row.

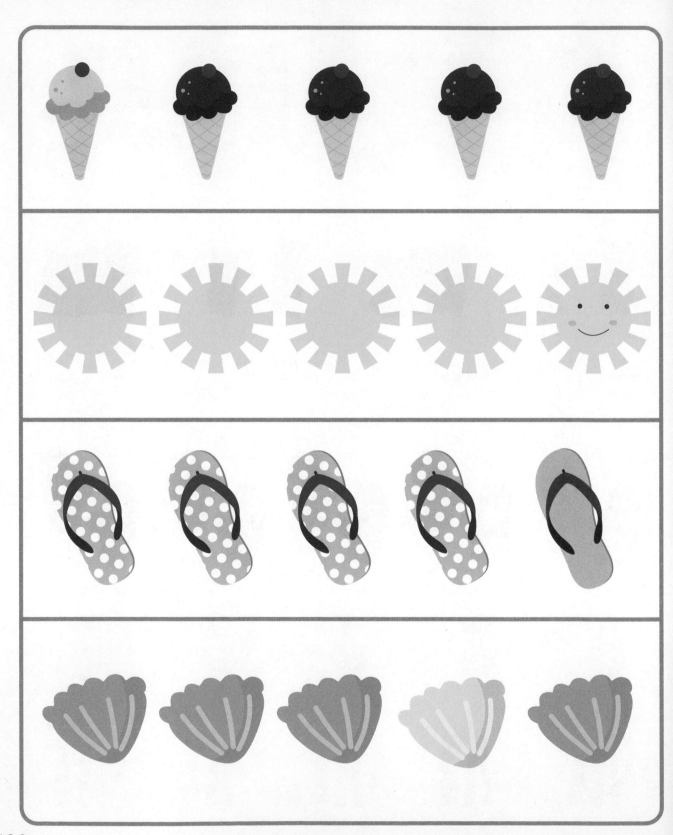

Sorting and Categorizing

One of the things in each row doesn't belong there.
Cross out the objects that don't belong.

Graphing Shapes

Color in the graph to show how many of each shape is in the picture below.

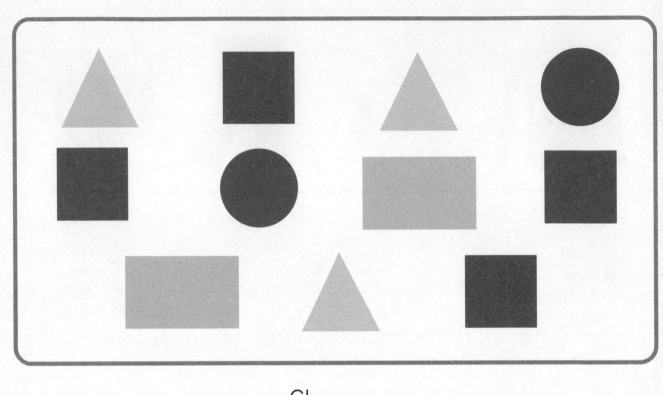

Shapes

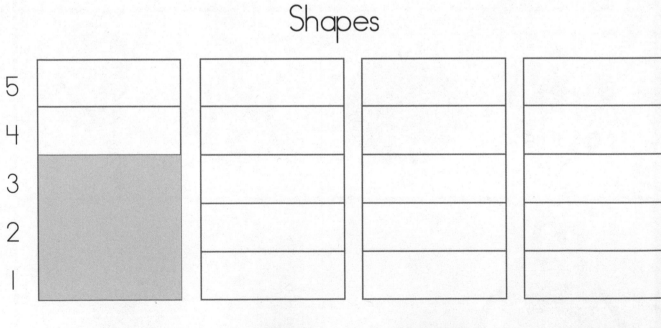

Reading a Bar Graph

Each colored section represents one person who likes that sport. Count how many votes each sport received and answer the questions below.

How many people like football?_____

How many people like soccer?_____

How many people like basketball?_____

How many people like baseball?_____

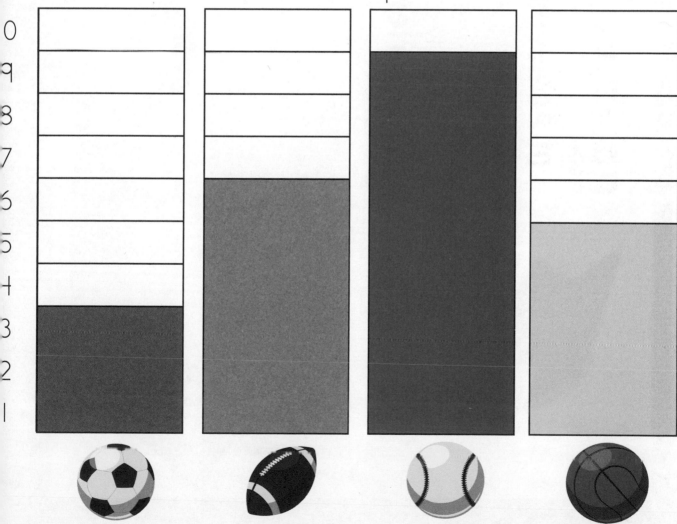

Our Favorite Sports

CERTIFICATE
of Achievement

....

has successfully completed **Kindergarten Math**

Signed: ....

Date: ....

Extra Practice Pages

Table of Contents

Making Words

Practice tracing the letters with your finger and saying the sentences and sounds of the letters below.

Then write the beginning sound for each word.

Remember: When reading the letters after each sentence, you should say the sound each letter makes, not the letter name.

Say, "Snake, snake, S...S...S," while making a slithery snake motion with your hand.

Say, "Apple, apple, A...A...A," while pretending to eat an apple.

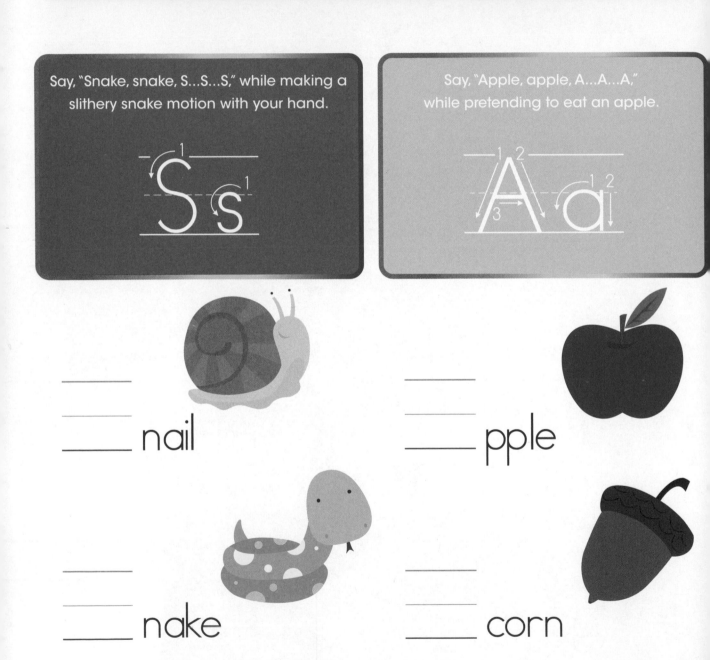

_____ nail

_____ pple

_____ nake

_____ corn

Making Words

Practice tracing the letters with your finger and saying the sentences and sounds of the letters below.

Then write the beginning sound for each word.

Remember: When reading the letters after each sentence, you should say the sound each letter makes, not the letter name.

Say, "Tiger, tiger, T...T...T," while making claws with your hands and roaring.

Say, "Iguana, iguana, I...I...I," while sticking your tongue out like an iguana.

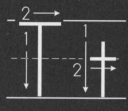

_____ urtle

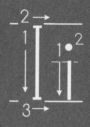

_____ guana

_____ iger

_____ sland

Making Words

Practice tracing the letters with your finger and saying the sentences and sounds of the letters below.

Then write the beginning sound for each word.

Remember: When reading the letters after each sentence, you should say the sound each letter makes, not the letter name.

Say, "Koala, koala, K...K...K," while pretending you're hugging a tree.

Say, "Night, night, N...N...N," while closing your eyes like you're pretending to sleep.

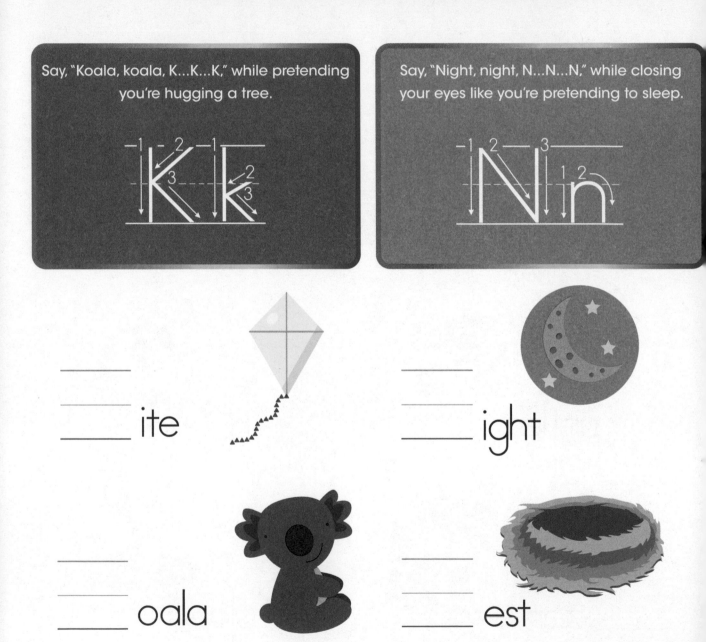

_____ ite

_____ ight

_____ oala

_____ est

Making Words

Practice tracing the letters with your finger and saying the sentences and sounds of the letters below.

Then write the beginning sound for each word.

Remember: When reading the letters after each sentence, you should say the sound each letter makes, not the letter name.

Say, "Crab, crab, C...C...C," while pretending to make crab claws with your hands.

Say, "Pig, pig, P...P...P," while scrunching your nose up like a pig.

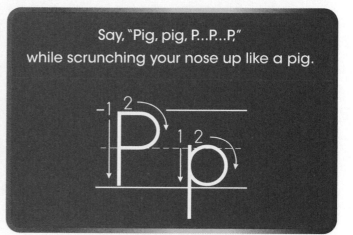

_____ at

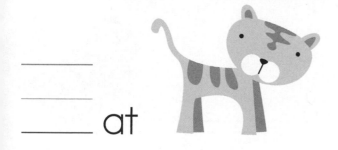

_____ ig

_____ oat

_____ ail

Making Words

Practice tracing the letters with your finger and saying the sentences and sounds of the letters below.

Then write the beginning sound for each word.

Remember: When reading the letters after each sentence, you should say the sound each letter makes, not the letter name.

Say, "Eagle, eagle, E...E...E," while bending your arms and flapping them like wings.

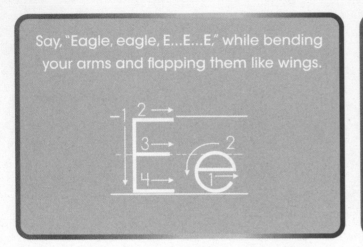

Say, "Hand, hand, H...H...H," while waving your hands high in the air.

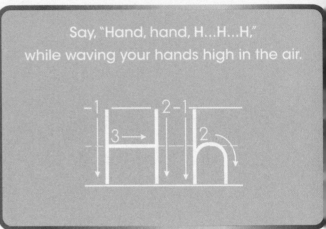

_____ agle

_____ eart

_____ gg

_____ orse

Making Words

Practice tracing the letters with your finger and saying the sentences and sounds of the letters below.

Then write the beginning sound for each word.

Remember: When reading the letters after each sentence, you should say the sound each letter makes, not the letter name.

Say, "Rabbit, rabbit, R...R...R," while making rabbit ears with your hands.

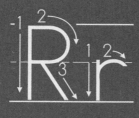

Say, "Monkey, monkey, M...M...M," while scratching yourself and bouncing around.

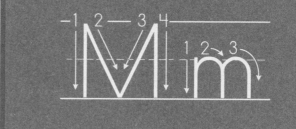

_____ obot

_____ oon

_____ abbit

_____ onkey

Making Words

Practice tracing the letters with your finger and saying the sentences and sounds of the letters below.

Then write the beginning sound for each word.

Remember: When reading the letters after each sentence, you should say the sound each letter makes, not the letter name.

Say, "Dog, dog, D...D...D," while barking like a dog.

Say, "Garden, garden G...G...G," while pretending to smell flowers you have picked.

_____ rum

_____ oat

_____ og

_____ arden

Making Words

Practice tracing the letters with your finger and saying the sentences and sounds of the letters below.

Then write the beginning sound for each word.

Remember: When reading the letters after each sentence, you should say the sound each letter makes, not the letter name.

Say, "Owl, owl, O...O...O," while flapping your arms like wings.

Say, "Lion, lion, L...L...L," while roaring and making your hands look like paws.

_____ wl

_____ ion

_____ ctopus

_____ izard

Making Words

Practice tracing the letters with your finger and saying the sentences and sounds of the letters below.

Then write the beginning sound for each word.

Remember: When reading the letters after each sentence, you should say the sound each letter makes, not the letter name.

Say, "Flower, flower, F...F...F,"
while opening your fingers like a flower.

Say, "Baby, baby, B...B...B,"
while pretending you're rocking a baby.

 ___ ish

 ___ oat

___ lower

___ all

Making Words

Practice tracing the letters with your finger and saying the sentences and sounds of the letters below.

Then write the beginning sound for each word.

Remember: When reading the letters after each sentence, you should say the sound each letter makes, not the letter name.

Say, "Queen, queen, Q...Q...Q," while pretending to put a crown on your head.

Say, "Unicorn, unicorn, U...U...U," while prancing like a unicorn.

_____ uail

_____ mbrella

_____ ueen

_____ nicorn

Making Words

Practice tracing the letters with your finger and saying the sentences and sounds of the letters below.

Then write the beginning sound for each word.

Remember: When reading the letters after each sentence, you should say the sound each letter makes, not the letter name.

Say, "Jump, jump, J...J...J," while jumping up and down.

Say, "Zebra, zebra, Z...Z...Z," while galloping like a zebra.

_____ uice

_____ ipper

_____ ump

_____ ebra

Making Words

Practice tracing the letters with your finger and saying the sentences and sounds of the letters below.

Then write the beginning sound for each word.

Remember: When reading the letters after each sentence, you should say the sound each letter makes, not the letter name.

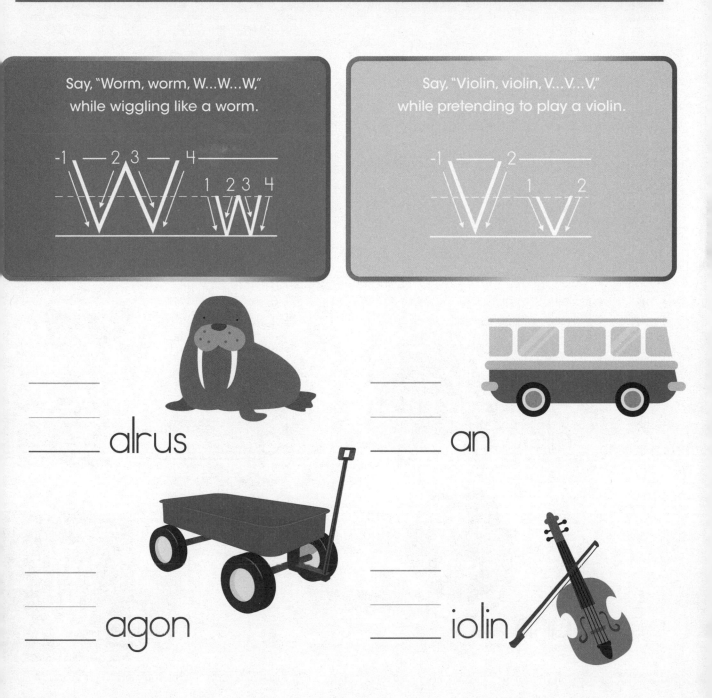

Say, "Worm, worm, W...W...W," while wiggling like a worm.

Say, "Violin, violin, V...V...V," while pretending to play a violin.

_____ alrus

_____ an

_____ agon

_____ iolin

Making Words

Practice tracing the letters with your finger and saying the sentences and sounds of the letters below.

Then write the beginning sound for each word.

Remember: When reading the letters after each sentence, you should say the sound each letter makes, not the letter name.

Say, "Yo-yo, yo-yo, Y...Y...Y," while pretending to play with a yo-yo.

Say, "X-ray, x-ray, X...X...X," while pretending to take an x-ray.

____ ak

fo ____

____ arn

____ -ray

Super Sight Words

Read the sight words in the clouds. Then find and circle the sight words in the box.

he   he   her   go

mom   is   dog   up

me   friend   is   she

and   up   she   me

tree   go   her   and

Super Sight Words

Sight words are words that we see a lot in books and often cannot be sounded out easily. Practice reading, writing, and spelling these words so you can read them the next time you see them.

a	I
said	**the**

Practice writing the sight words on the lines below.

a

the

said

Super Sight Words

Sight words are words that we see a lot in books and often cannot be sounded out easily. Practice reading, writing, and spelling these words so you can read them the next time you see them.

can

has

like

am

Complete each sentence using a sight word from above.

_____

I _____ rabbits.

I _____ jump rope.

She _____ a new bike.

Which Word?

Say each sound in the words and blend the sounds together.
Circle the correct word below each picture and then color the pictures.

cat   cap

peg   pig

sit   six

dog   dig

jug   jog

beg   bug

Which Word?

Say each sound in the words and blend the sounds together.
Circle the correct word below each picture and then color the pictures.

hit   hat   bed   bad

fog   frog   bat   bet

her   hen   tan   ten

Trace the numbers 1 and 2 and the words one and two with your pencil. Then practice writing the numbers and words.

Color the three apples red. Count the total number of apples. Then color the picture.

Trace the numbers 3 and 4 and the words three and four with your pencil. Then practice writing the numbers and words.

Someone forgot the birthday candles! Draw three candles on top of the birthday cake.

Where are the pizza toppings? Draw four of your favorite toppings on the pizza.

Trace the numbers 5 and 6 and the words five and six with your pencil. Then practice writing the numbers and words.

Count and color the frogs in the pond. How many frogs are there?

Trace the numbers 7 and 8 and the words seven and eight with your pencil. Then practice writing the numbers and words.

Draw lines to the correct pails where Julia will put each group of shells to add to her seashell collection.

Know Your Numbers

Trace the numbers 9 and 10 and the words nine and ten with your pencil. Then practice writing the numbers and words.

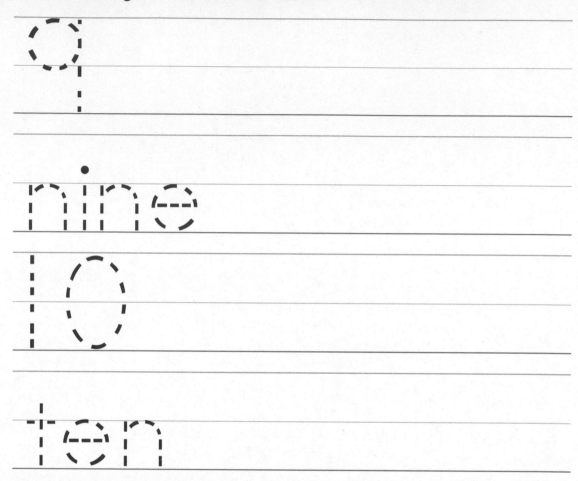

Draw a line from the sets of circus objects to the matching numbers on the signs.

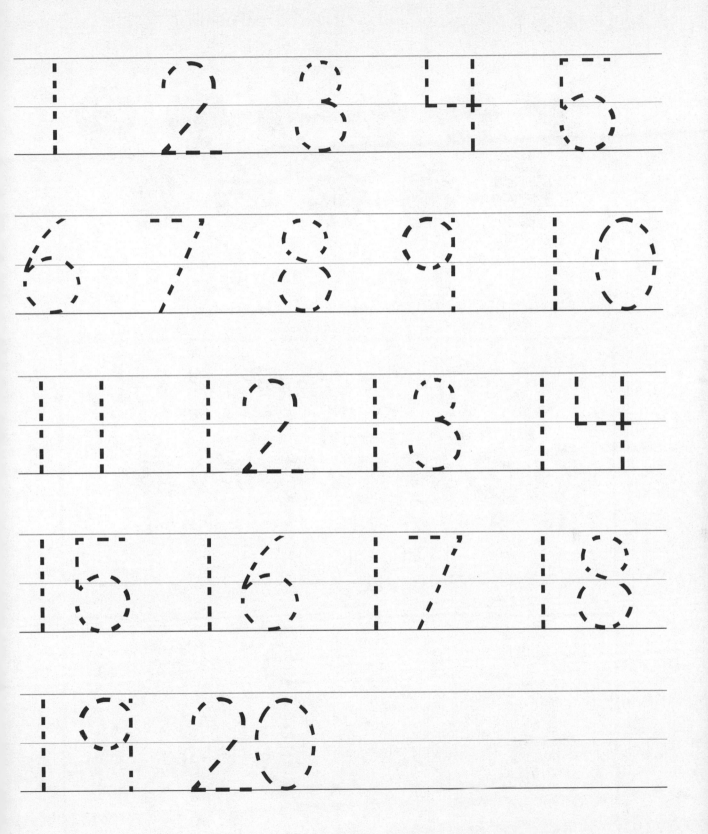

Crazy Counting

Count the objects in each box and circle the correct number.

11   12   13   14   15

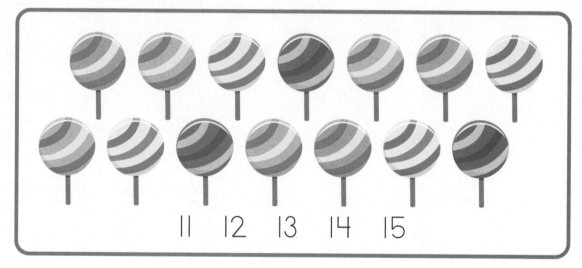

11   12   13   14   15

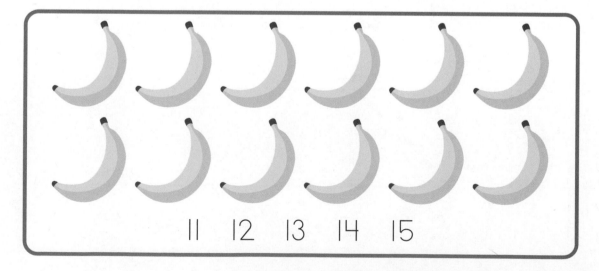

11   12   13   14   15

Crazy Counting

Count the objects in each box and circle the correct number.

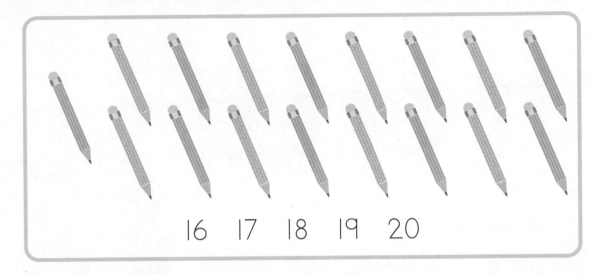

16   17   18   19   20

11   12   13   14   15

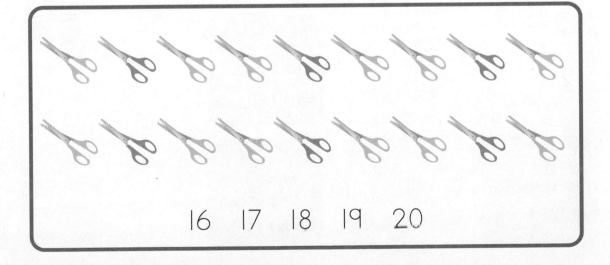

16   17   18   19   20

Before and After

Spring has sprung! It is time to water the flowers. Write the numbers that come before and after the number on each watering can in the boxes below.

Spring has sprung! It is time to water the flowers. Write the numbers that come before and after the number on each watering can in the boxes below.

Cool Clocks

A clock has the numbers 1 to 12 on its face. Look at the clock below. Some numbers are missing! Fill in the missing numbers.

The short hand is pointing to the 2, so it is 2 o'clock.

Cool Clocks

Look at the short hand on each of the clocks
and write the time next to each one.

_____ o'clock

_____ o'clock

_____ o'clock

Trace the uppercase and lowercase letters with your finger. Then practice tracing and writing them below.

Letter Practice

Trace the uppercase and lowercase letters with your finger. Then practice tracing and writing them below.

Trace the uppercase and lowercase letters with your finger. Then practice tracing and writing them below.

Trace the uppercase and lowercase letters with your finger. Then practice tracing and writing them below.

Trace the uppercase and lowercase letters with your finger. Then practice tracing and writing them below.

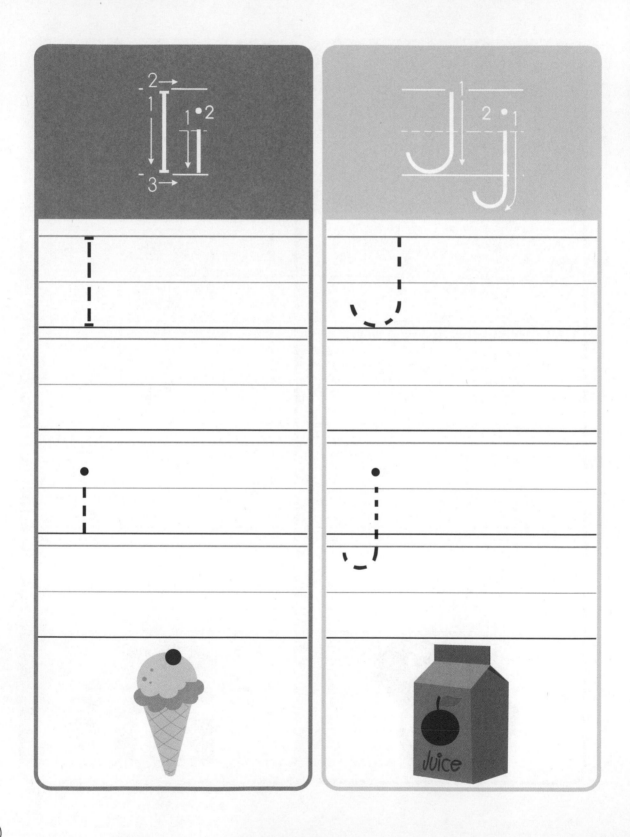

Trace the uppercase and lowercase letters with your finger. Then practice tracing and writing them below.

Trace the uppercase and lowercase letters with your finger. Then practice tracing and writing them below.

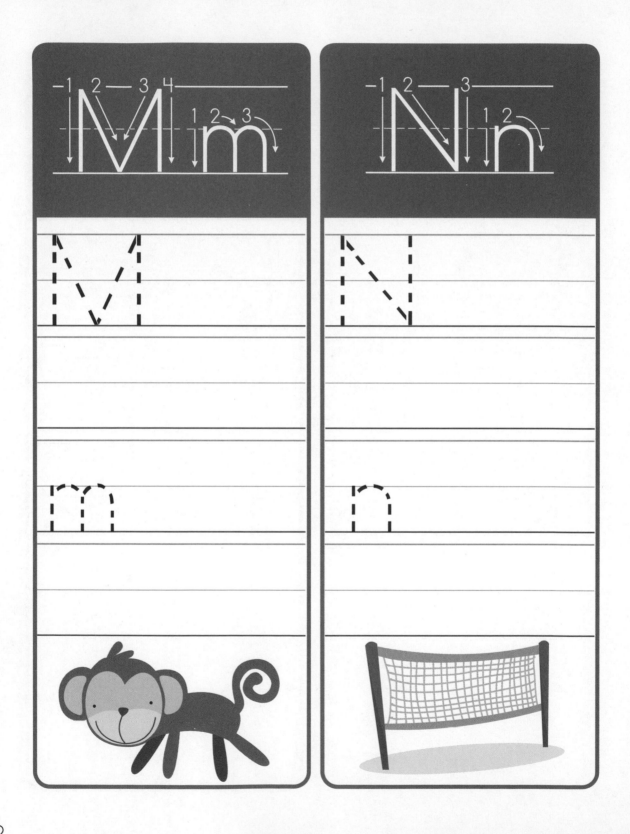

Trace the uppercase and lowercase letters with your finger. Then practice tracing and writing them below.

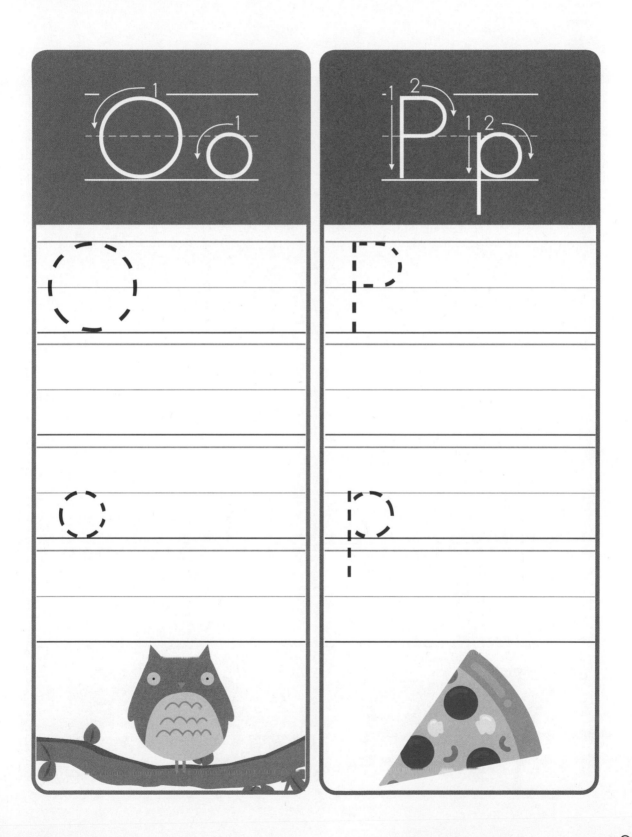

Trace the uppercase and lowercase letters with your finger. Then practice tracing and writing them below.

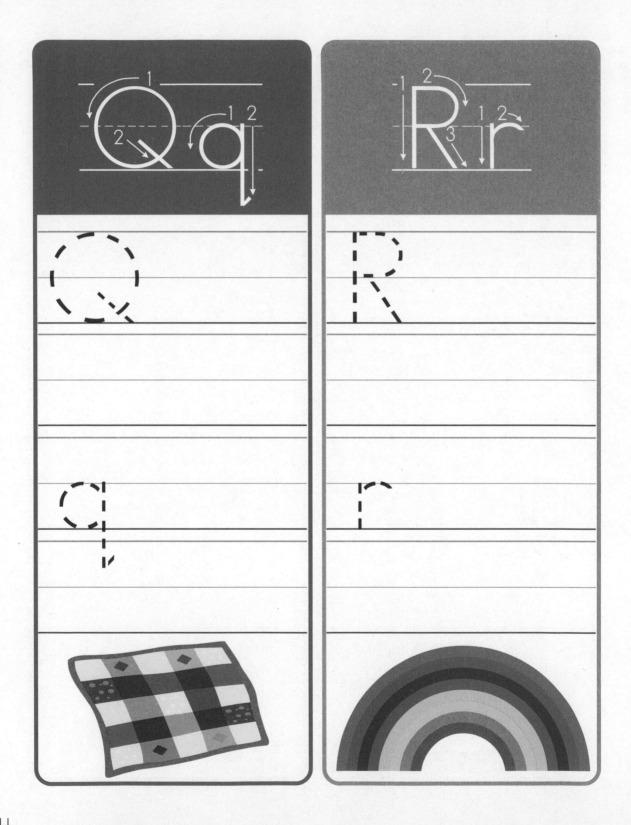

Trace the uppercase and lowercase letters with your finger. Then practice tracing and writing them below.

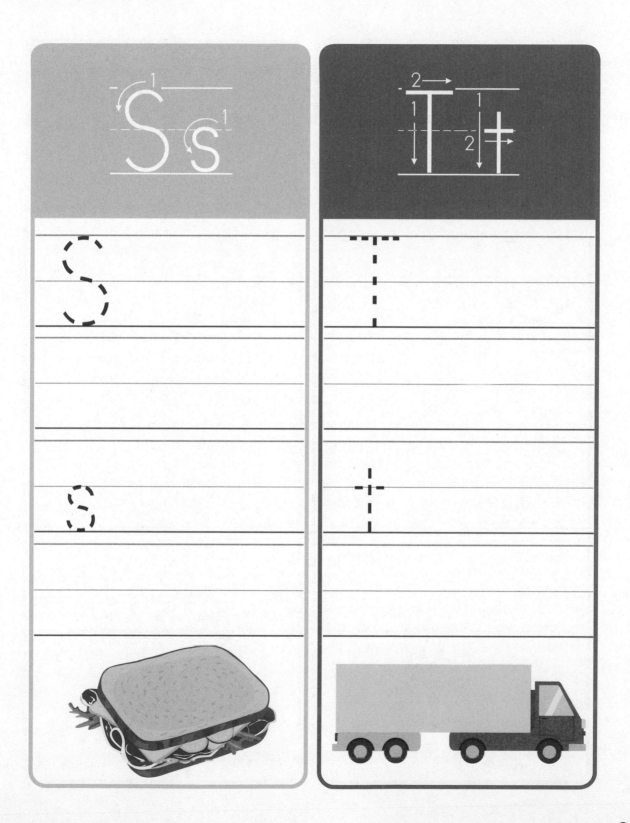

Letter Practice

Trace the uppercase and lowercase letters with your finger. Then practice tracing and writing them below.

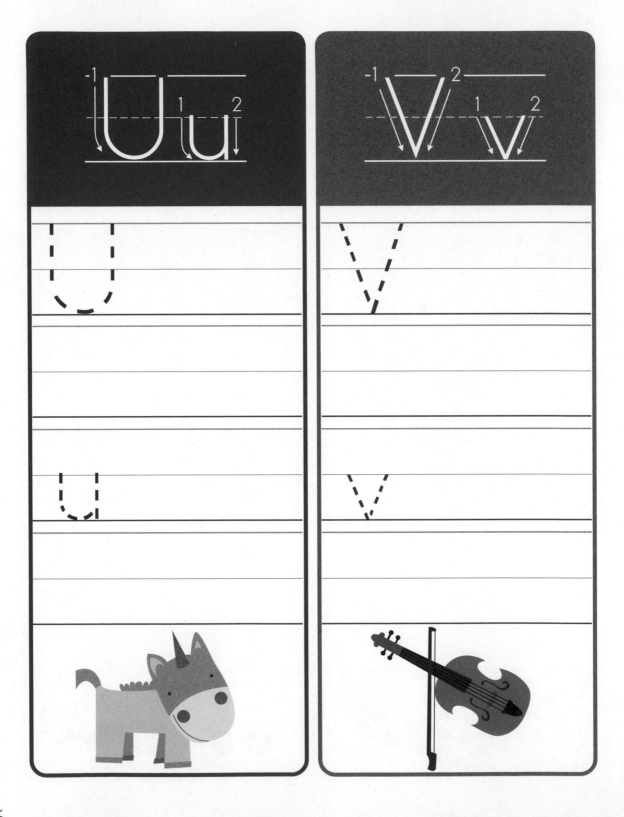

Letter Practice

Trace the uppercase and lowercase letters with your finger. Then practice tracing and writing them below.

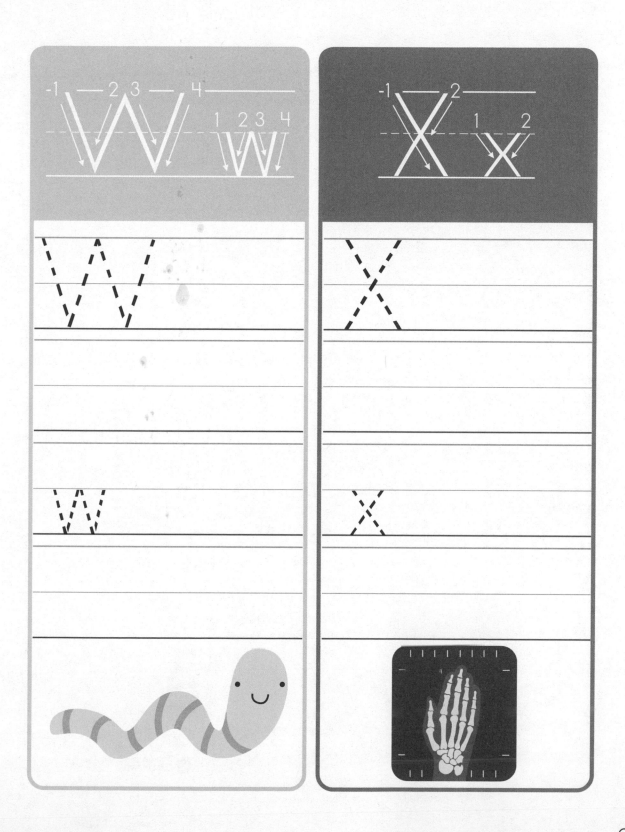

Trace the uppercase and lowercase letters with your finger. Then practice tracing and writing them below.

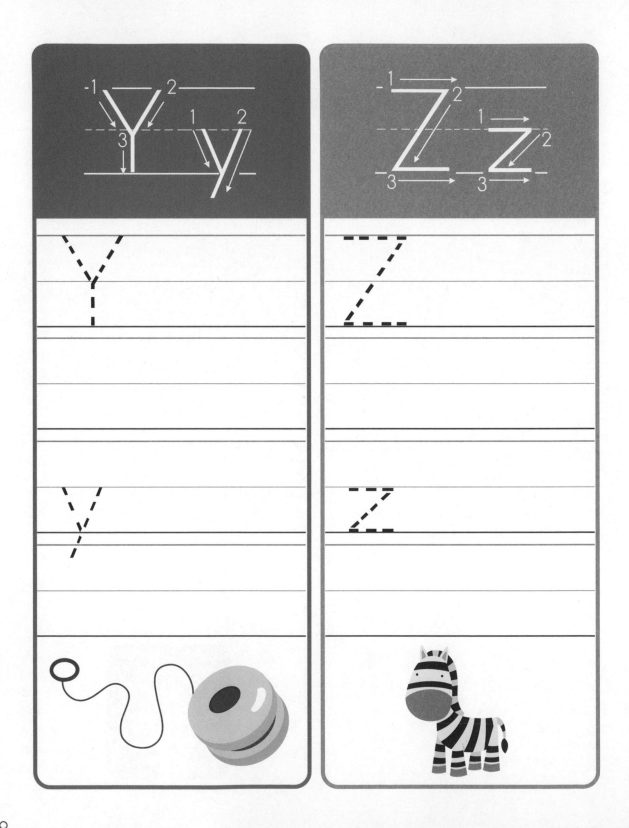

Letter Tracing

Practice writing the alphabet by tracing the uppercase and lowercase letters.

I Am a Writer

Writers like to write about their favorite people, animals, places, and things. Write about your favorite animal or place on the lines below.

Writers write about what they think. Remember to use the word "because" to link what you like to your reason for liking it. Write your opinion about what you like better on the lines below.

playing

or

reading

_____

_____

_____

_____

_____

_____

_____

ANSWER KEY

Page 31

Write the missing letter combination for each word below.

sh ip   fi sh   ba th

Page 32

Write the beginning letter combination for each word below.

wh eel   ch eek   wh ale

Page 37

-at
What words are in the -at word family?

Build new words with the -at word family. Fill in the missing letters to complete the words. Then color the pictures.

C at

m at

h at

b at

r at

Page 39

-op
What words are in the -op word family?

Build new words with the -op word family. Fill in the missing letters to complete the words on the -op train.

m op   t op

p op   h op

Page 41

-ug
What words are in the -ug word family?

Build new words with the -ug word family. Fill in the missing letters to complete the words. Then color the pictures.

b ug

r ug

j ug

m ug

h ug

Page 43

-ot
What words are in the -ot word family?

Build new words with the -ot word family. Color the pictures that show words that have the -ot sound in them. Look for hot, dot, and pot.

Page 45

Beginning Sound and Letter
What beginning sound do you hear? Write the beginning letter that matches both pictures on the lines below.

s

l

p

m

c

Page 46

Middle Sounds
Say the word for each picture. Listen for the sound you hear in the middle. Circle the letter that makes that sound.

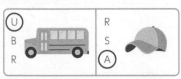

U / B / R   R / S / A

N / O / Y   T / I / L

P / E / R   F / I / U

Page 47

Ending Sounds
Say the word for each picture. Listen for the sound you hear at the end. Write the letter that makes that sound on the lines below.

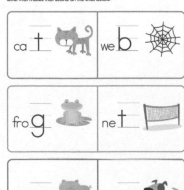

ca t   we b

fro g   ne t

pi g   do g

Page 49

Match the Rhymes
Draw a line to match the words that rhyme. Then color the pictures.

Sun   Fan
Wish   Mop
Pan   Wig
Top   Fun
Pig   Fish

Page 50

Reading Rhymes

Find the Rhyme
Circle the picture that rhymes with the picture on the left.

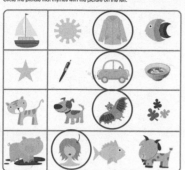

Write a word on the lines below that rhymes with the picture.

_____

Page 51

Reading Rhymes

Find the Rhyme
Circle the words in the picture that rhyme with the word hat. Then color the hat.

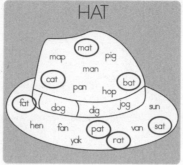

Write a word on the lines below that rhymes with the picture.

_____

Page 57

Sight Word Games

Follow the directions below.

Read the sight words.

see   like   me   the   to

Find and circle the sight words below.

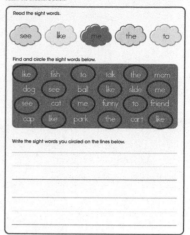

Write the sight words you circled on the lines below.

_____
_____
_____
_____

Page 58

Sight Word Games

Practice writing sight words on the lines below.

look _____

like _____

play _____

Write the sight words from above in the sentences below.

I **like** dogs!

I can **look** out the window.

Will you come and **play** with me?

Page 59

Sight Word Games

Color the picture using the key below.

green = and   blue = see   red = me
purple = to   orange = up   yellow = no

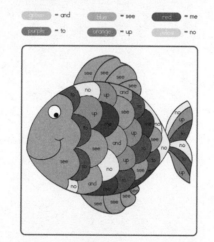

Page 60

Understanding What I Read

It is important that a child understands what she or he is reading, even from a young age. Ask your child questions about what is happening in the story as you read. Reading and talking about what you read can become a great way to connect with your child.

Time to Read!

Read the sentences below. Then circle the correct answers to the questions about the sentences.

I like to eat apples.
They are good for me.

1. What do you like to eat?
   • I like to eat apples.
   • I like to eat oranges.
2. Why do you eat them?
   • They are sweet.
   • They are good for me.

Page 61

Understanding What I Read

Time to Read!

Read the sentences below. Then circle the correct answers to the questions about the sentences.

I can go out to play.
It is fun!

1. What can you do?
   • I can go out to play.
   • I can ride a bike.
2. Why do you play?
   • I like it.
   • It is fun!

Page 62

Understanding What I Read

Time to Read!

Read the sentences below. Then circle the correct answers to the questions about the sentences.

I see a dog.
The dog ran away.

1. What do you see?
   • I see a cat.
   • I see a dog.
2. What did the dog do?
   • The dog ran away.
   • The dog barked.

Page 63

Understanding What I Read

Time to Read!

Read the sentences below. Then circle the correct answers to the questions about the sentences.

We are at the beach.
I'm playing in the sand.

1. Where are we?
   • We are at school.
   • We are at the beach.
2. What are you doing?
   • I'm playing in the sand.
   • I'm swimming.

Page 120

Matching Uppercase and Lowercase

Using your favorite crayon, draw a line from the uppercase letter to the matching lowercase letter.

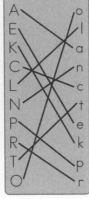

Page 129

Understanding Numbers Game

Make your way from the car to the campground by following the path of numbers 1-20 in the correct order. Make sure to point to each number as you say it!

Page 131

Understanding Numbers 1-5

Count the insects and write the number 1 and the word one the lines below.

Page 133

Understanding Numbers 1-5

Practice writing the number 2 on the lines below.

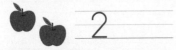

2

Circle the set of two apples below.

Page 135

Understanding Numbers 1-5

Circle each set of three dogs. Practice writing the number 3 on the lines below.

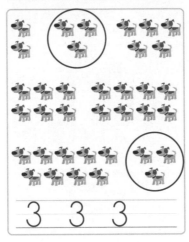

Page 137

Understanding Numbers 1-5

Where are the chocolate chips? Draw four chocolate chips on the cookie. Practice writing the number 4 on the lines below.

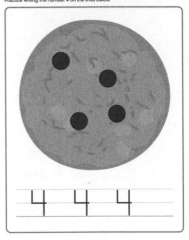

Page 139

Understanding Numbers 1-5

How many swans are in the pond? Count the swans. Then color the swans and write the number on the lines below.

Page 140

Counting Numbers 1-5

Count the objects and write the number and the word on the lines below.

Page 141

Counting Numbers 1-5

Trace the numbers below. Then draw a line from the number to the matching set of objects.

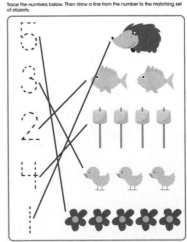

Page 143

Understanding Numbers 6–10

Count the animals and write the number on the lines below.

6

6

6

6

Page 145

Understanding Numbers 6–10

Practice writing the number 7 on the lines below.

7

Circle each set of seven fruits below.

Page 147

Understanding Numbers 6–10

Circle each set of eight cats. Practice writing the number 8 on the lines below.

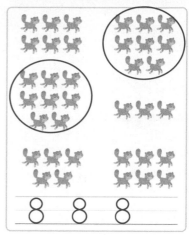

8   8   8

Page 149

Understanding Numbers 6–10

Where are the balloons? Draw nine balloons on top of the strings. Practice writing the number 9 on the lines below.

9   9   9

Page 151

Understanding Numbers 6–10

How many leaves are on the tree? Count the leaves. Then color the leaves and write the number on the lines below.

10

Page 152

Counting Numbers 6–10

Count the vehicles and write the number on the lines below.

6

7

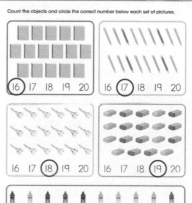
8

9

10

Page 153

Counting Numbers 6–10

Trace the numbers below. Then draw a line from the number to the matching set of objects.

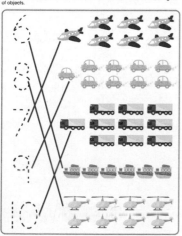

Page 155

Understanding Numbers 11–20

Count the objects and circle the correct number below each set of pictures.

(11) 12 13 14 15   11 (12) 13 14 15

11 12 (13) 14 15   11 12 13 (14) 15

11 12 13 14 (15)

Page 157

Understanding Numbers 11–20

Count the objects and circle the correct number below each set of pictures.

(16) 17 18 19 20   16 (17) 18 19 20

16 17 (18) 19 20   16 17 18 (19) 20

16 17 18 19 (20)

Page 160

Adding Numbers 1–10

Point to and count the red dots. Write the number on the lines below. Count the blue dots and write the number on the lines below. How many red and blue dots are there in all? Write the number on the lines below.

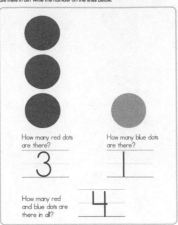

How many red dots are there?
3

How many blue dots are there?
1

How many red and blue dots are there in all?
4

Page 161

Adding Numbers 1–10

Point to and count the seashells on the beach. Write the number on the lines below. Count how many sandcastles there are and write the number on the lines below. How many seashells and sandcastles are there in all? Write the number on the lines below.

How many seashells are there?
2

How many sandcastles are there?
2

How many seashells and sandcastles are there in all?
4

Page 162

Adding Numbers 1–10

Point to and count the green blocks you see. Write the number on the lines below. Count how many yellow blocks there are and write the number on the lines below. How many green and yellow blocks are there in all? Write the number on the lines below.

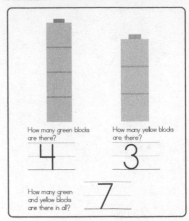

How many green blocks are there?
4

How many yellow blocks are there?
3

How many green and yellow blocks are there in all?
7

Page 163

Adding Numbers 1–10

Point to and count the frogs you can see. Write the number on the lines below. Count how many lily pads there are and write the number on the lines below. How many frogs and lily pads are there in all? Write the number on the lines below.

How many frogs are there?
5

How many lily pads are there?
5

How many frogs and lily pads are there in all?
10

Page 164

Subtracting Numbers 1–10

Point to and count all of the cats in the picture. Write the number on the lines below. Cross out the gray cats. How many gray cats did you cross out? How many cats are left? Write the numbers on the lines below.

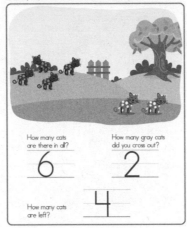

How many cats are there in all?
6

How many gray cats did you cross out?
2

How many cats are left?
4

Page 165

Subtracting Numbers 1–10

Point to and count all of the cubes below. Write the number on the lines below. Cross out the blue cubes. How many blue cubes did you cross out? How many cubes are left? Write the numbers on the lines below.

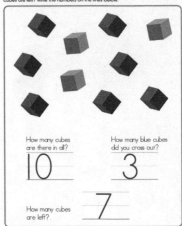

How many cubes are there in all?
10

How many blue cubes did you cross out?
3

How many cubes are left?
7

Page 166

Subtracting Numbers 1–10

Point to and count all of the deer in the picture. Write the number on the lines below. Cross out the deer without spots. How many deer without spots did you cross out? How many deer are left? Write the numbers on the lines below.

How many deer are there in all?
7

How many deer without spots did you cross out?
2

How many deer are left?
5

Page 167

Subtracting Numbers 1–10

Point to and count all of the circles. Write the number on the lines below. Cross out the yellow circles. How many yellow circles did you cross out? How many circles are left? Write the numbers on the lines below.

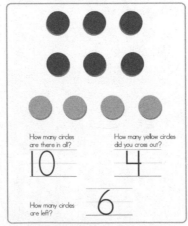

How many circles are there in all?
10

How many yellow circles did you cross out?
4

How many circles are left?
6

Page 169

Shapes

Name That Shape!
Circle the correct name of the shapes below.

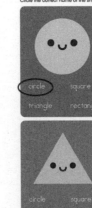

circle square
triangle rectangle

circle square
triangle rectangle

circle square
triangle rectangle

circle square
triangle rectangle

236

Page 170

Shapes

Count the shapes in the picture. Write the number of each shape on the lines below. Then color the shapes.

5 circles   3 squares
8 rectangles   1 triangle

Page 171

Shapes

Shape Jumble!

Color Key
Circle:	Red	Square:	Green
Rectangle:	Blue	Triangle:	Orange

Color the shapes below using the color key.

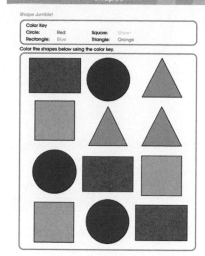

Page 173

Understanding Measurement

Longer and Shorter
Circle the objects that are longer. Cross out the objects that are shorter.

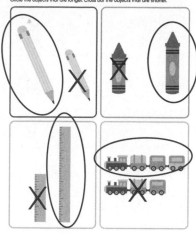

Page 174

Understanding Measurement

Bigger and Smaller
Circle the objects that are bigger. Cross out the objects that are smaller.

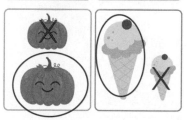

Page 175

Understanding Measurement

Heavier and Lighter
Circle the objects that are heavier. Cross out the objects that are lighter.

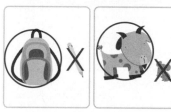

Page 176

Understanding Time

What time is it? Some things happen during the day and some things happen at night. Draw a line from the time of day to the matching picture.

Daytime

Nighttime

Page 177

Understanding Time

Let's Talk About a Clock!
A clock has numbers from 1 to 12 on its face. Complete the picture of the clock by writing the missing numbers in the circles.

Page 179

Sorting and Categorizing

Same
Circle the objects that are the same in each row.

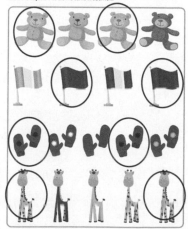

Page 180

Sorting and Categorizing

Different
Cross out the objects that are different in each row.

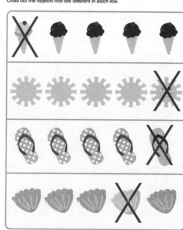

Page 181

One of the things in each row doesn't belong there.
Cross out the objects that don't belong.

55

Page 182

Graphing Shapes
Color in the graph to show how many of each shape is in the picture below.

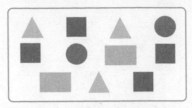

Shapes

56

Page 183

Reading a Bar Graph
Each colored section represents one person who likes that sport. Count how many votes each sport received and answer the questions below.

How many people like football? __6__

How many people like soccer? __3__

How many people like basketball? __5__

How many people like baseball? __9__

Our Favorite Sports

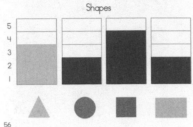

57

Page 199

Read the sight words in the clouds. Then find and circle the sight words in the box.

Page 201

Sight words are words that we see a lot in books and often cannot be sounded out easily. Practice reading, writing, and spelling these words so you can read them the next time you see them.

Page 202

Say each sound in the words and blend the sounds together.
Circle the correct word below each picture and then color the pictures.

Page 203

Say each sound in the words and blend the sounds together.
Circle the correct word below each picture and then color the pictures.

Page 207

Trace the numbers 7 and 8 and the words seven and eight with your pencil.
Then practice writing the numbers and words.

Draw lines to the correct pails where Julia will put each group of shells to add to her seashell collection.

Page 208

Trace the numbers 9 and 10 and the words nine and ten with your pencil.
Then practice writing the numbers and words.

Draw a line from the sets of circus objects to the matching numbers on the signs.

238

Page 210

Crazy Counting

Count the objects in each box and circle the correct number.

11 (11) 12 13 14 15

11 12 13 (14) 15

11 (12) 13 14 15

Page 211

Crazy Counting

Count the objects in each box and circle the correct number.

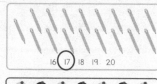

16 (17) 18 19 20

11 12 (13) 14 15

16 17 (18) 19 20

Page 212

Before and After

Spring has sprung! It is time to water the flowers. Write the numbers that come before and after the number on each watering can in the boxes below.

5	6	7
8	9	10
2	3	4
11	12	13
13	14	15
15	16	17

Page 213

Before and After

Spring has sprung! It is time to water the flowers. Write the numbers that come before and after the number on each watering can in the boxes below.

4	5	6
9	10	11
1	2	3
7	8	9
12	13	14
18	19	20

Page 214

Cool Clocks

A clock has the numbers 1 to 12 on its face. Look at the clock on the left. Some numbers are missing! Fill in the missing numbers.

The short hand is pointing to the 2, so it is 2 o'clock.

Page 215

Cool Clocks

Look at the short hand on each of the clocks and write the time next to each one.

7 o'clock

5 o'clock

3 o'clock

239

Build Solid Foundations for Learning

Workbooks

Pre-Kindergarten Reading Workbook

Kindergarten Reading Workbook

First Grade Reading Workbook

Pre-Kindergarten Writing Workbook

Kindergarten Writing Workbook

First Grade Writing Workbook

Pre-Kindergarten Math Workbook

Kindergarten Math Workbook

First Grade Math Workbook

Collections

Pre-Kindergarten Workbook · Reading · Writing · Math

Kindergarten Workbook · Reading · Writing · Math

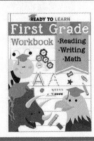
First Grade Workbook · Reading · Writing · Math

Workpads

Pre-Kindergarten READY TO LEARN Skill-Building Workpad

Kindergarten READY TO LEARN Skill-Building Workpad

First Grade READY TO LEARN Skill-Building Workpad

Flash Cards

Alphabet Flash Cards

Numbers Flash Cards

Sight Words Flash Cards

3-Letter Words Flash Cards

Addition Flash Cards

Subtraction Flash Cards